NEW SCIENCE LIBRARY

presents traditional topics from a modern perspective, particularly those associated with the hard sciences—physics, biology, and medicine—and those of the human sciences—psychology, sociology, and philosophy.

The aim of this series is the enrichment of both the scientific and spiritual view of the world through their mutual dialogue and exchange.

New Science Library is an imprint of Shambhala Publications.

General editor Ken Wilber

Consulting editors Jeremy Hayward
Francisco Varela

EVOLUTION

The Grand Synthesis

Ervin Laszlo

FOREWORD BY JONAS SALK

NEW SCIENCE LIBRARY
SHAMBHALA / Boston & London
1987

New Science Library
An imprint of
Shambhala Publications, Inc.
314 Dartmouth Street
Boston, Massachusetts 02116

9 8 7 6 5 4 3 2 1

FIRST EDITION

Printed in the United States of America

Distributed in the United States by Random House
and in Canada by Random House of Canada Ltd.

Library of Congress Cataloging-in-Publication Data
Laszlo, Ervin, 1932–
  Evolution, the grand synthesis.

  Bibliography: p.
  Includes index.
  1. Evolution.   2. Social evolution.   I. Title.
QH371.L37   1987   116   86-17805
ISBN 0-87773-389-9 (pbk.)

For Carita

Contents

Preface

by ALEXANDER KING, President of the Club of Rome

It is not infrequently that the probings of scientific research appear to provide substance to the vaguely stated concepts of ancient philosophers, which were essentially intuitive or speculative comments on the nature of things. Proof of the existence of atoms a century ago was a case in point, while later elucidation of their microcosmic structures immediately suggested analogies with the macrocosmos of the universe.

Two other ancient concepts—"As above, so below" and "All the world is of a piece and only the blindness of man obscures the essential oneness of it"—seem to have acquired particular significance today, illuminated by the discoveries of fundamental research and observation of social systems.

In this important and ambitious book Ervin Laszlo approaches the unification of knowledge, and indeed of universal and planetary existence, not on mere analogies but on the basis of the recent discoveries of nonequilibrium thermodynamics with its concept of bifurcation and of other work on the dynamics of change in complex systems. He concentrates his arguments on a generalized concept of the process of evolution as it is manifest, inter alia, in cosmic, biological, and social systems. He makes a strong plea for the grand evolutionary synthesis and provides an approach to its elaboration. This synthesis rests on the proposition that the course of evolution, however chaotic it may appear to be, is subject to general laws that can be applied to physical, biological, ecological, and social systems. Laszlo stresses that a new paradigm is emerging in many fields of science, leading to a replacement of earlier ideas that were based on mechanistic determinacy and the attractions of static equilibria, toward new models of change, indeterminacy, and nonequilibria. We have seen recently, in the work of Ilya Prigogine and his school, the application of such ideas to a wide variety of biological systems, far beyond those of nonequilibrium thermodynamics from which the new concepts were derived. Ervin Laszlo generalizes this and related approaches toward a grand evolutionary synthesis. He insists that the new approach is essentially optimistic. Evolution, he says, is not destiny: it is opportunity. Its path is not predictable, but it can be controlled.

The application of these ideas to discontinuous social change is particularly interesting. We have entered a situation of major discontinuity in human affairs, which Laszlo terms a "catastrophic bifurcation," and which I name The Great Transition. It has been caused by the upsurge of a revolutionary technology combined with the perturbation of two world wars. It is marked by an explosion of world population, the loss of traditional values, the destabilization of whole societies, widespread unemployment and change in the nature of employment, the globalization of problems and the obsolescence of institutions, political systems, and ideologies, as well as a whole range of other manifestations. This transformation will lead to an entirely different type of society throughout the world—for better or for worse according to our will and our capacity to master it.

Evidently, therefore, one of the great needs of our time is to develop means for the mastery of complexity and uncertainty, which will dominate governance for decades to come. *Evolution* does not pretend to provide all the answers, but it does offer valuable new insights that will greatly enhance the understanding of those who will guide us through the transition.

The discussion of the mastery of social change is particularly significant. The transition toward a global society is seen, not in simplistic federalist terms but as a convergence process, based on common self-interest and *collective* self-reliance in which de facto loss of elements of national sovereignty is accepted for practical advantages without de jure negation of sovereignty, that is, with preservation of national identity.

The thinking of the Club of Rome is centered on the concept of the "world problematique," a realization that the problems and hence the activities of humanity constitute an untidy tangle of interrelated and interacting issues. Hence, in attempting to provide a solution for a particular problem, we must anticipate and identify the consequences of the proposed solution on all other elements of the problematique. This concept is also the thinking of *Evolution*. We greatly welcome this book as an addition to the *Information Series of the Club of Rome: Contributions to the Understanding of the World Problematique*.

Foreword

by JONAS SALK

In this book Ervin Laszlo has turned his integrating mind to the task of bringing together observations that reveal the operation of the laws of nature in evolving emergent systems of increasing complexity. It is evident that we, as human beings, are here as a product of the process of evolution, and that everything is in evolution, including the reality of our own lives. For this reason it is necessary for us to turn our attention to understanding the process by which we have emerged and to reflect upon our selves not only as a product of the process but as a part of the process itself. By the freedom that we possess as coauthors of the process of evolution great responsibility is placed upon us.

Thus, nature and human nature, or nature and human beings, are at a stage in the long history of evolution at which there is a need for reconciliation if human evolution is to continue as long into the future as the life of the sun will permit. However, before this limit is reached there is a need to learn how to reconcile differences among groups in ways that prove to be mutually advantageous. For this we need to understand the phenomenon of evolution itself so that we may then, in due course, understand ourselves and the role we play in the inevitability that is implied by coauthorship in the process of our own evolution.

Can we come to terms with the inexorability of evolution itself—with all of the diversity in nature and in human nature—a process that generates and then consumes what it generates? If ever we are to succeed in such reconciliation it will be necessary that we become aware of the way evolution works and how it is manifest at all levels of complexity from atoms to cells to persons as well as before and beyond each. We will have to develop not only knowledge about but a feeling for the phenomenon itself, which we can do by observing it in all of its many manifestations and by experiencing it in our own lives.

The grand sweep of evolution over the expanse of time that has thus far elapsed is revealed in this book in a form that is useful for the nonscientist and the scientist alike. It is written for those from the two cultures as well as for each of the many cultures of both scientists and nonscientists who need to become informed about this most important phenomenon of nature that has so accelerated and is now having so direct a qualitative effect on our lives and on our destiny.

There is emerging a new literature on the subject of evolution, one that has expanded far beyond the limits of the work of Darwin and Wallace, who first made us aware of evolution and the origin of species. Since then evolution has come to be seen in a wider context. It is now seen in its universality, in its universal presence, and in its absence, as when species cease to evolve and are no longer able to persist. We now see the meaning of this in the human realm with the emergence of the capacity to evolve as the most valuable of all human attributes.

It is for this reason that we need to understand evolution fundamentally if we are to be able to maintain our place in the evolutionary scheme of things as an evolving species, as the first species that has the capacity to become part of the process and to persist in the process of evolution as long as we are able to evolve successfully.

If ever we are to be able to do so it will be because we have learned from nature and from evolution both nature's game and the game of evolution, in both of which we will have to become skilled, even more skilled and wiser than we have as yet demonstrated.

This book will help make us aware of the awesome challenge that this turn of events presents to us and to future generations. Can we rise to it? Time will tell. Do we have enough time? I presume that we do, provided we don't waste it. That's the meaning of the surge in interest in evolution in our time to which this useful, comprehensive, and illuminating book is a response.

Acknowledgments

The intellectual debt I owe for this book has roots deep in the history of systematic thought: it includes Whitehead no less than Darwin, Thales as well as Einstein. This debt cannot be fully measured, nor can it be satisfactorily acknowledged, for it has been accumulated over nearly three decades of study, reflection, and discussion. The writings that have influenced my thinking the most crucially are indicated in the Bibliography appended to this volume; it is to their authors that I owe whatever courage and inspiration the present study may possess.

But I do wish to briefly describe and acknowledge here the influences of the immediate context in which this book was conceived, written, and time after time revised and rewritten. I should begin, perhaps, by recalling a happy encounter with Erich Jantsch at a conference in 1974 in Tokyo. Following an initial discussion and comparison of our conceptions of self-organizing systems, I gave him a copy of my recently published *Introduction to Systems Philosophy,* and he lent me his latest, just completed and as yet untitled manuscript. We retired to our rooms and had finished reading by 5:00 A.M. and met again for breakfast. From this initial exchange came a synthesis, in my mind and, I believe, also in his, of his more quantitative orientation based on the works of Ilya Prigogine and his own work in planning and organization theory, with my more qualitative perspective derived from Bergson, Whitehead, and above all from Ludwig von Bertalanffy. Within a year I was able to publish his manuscript, titled *Design for Evolution,* in the International Library of Systems Theory and Philosophy, which I then edited. Our contacts did not cease: some years later, following a close collaboration in the preparation of the final text, I was pleased to include the *Self-Organizing Universe* in the Systems Science and World Order Library, a new series I founded in the interim.

Jantsch introduced me to Prigogine and his Brussels collaborators. Following the impact of my earlier close collaboration with von Bertalanffy, it was Prigogine and his work that came to exert the strongest influence on my thinking. Convinced of the applicability of the irreversible dynamics of nonequilibrium dissipative systems to the biological and even to the social worlds, I could prevail on Prigogine to produce a study extending systematic consideration to biological species, ecosystems, and sociocultural evolution itself. Authored by Prigogine jointly with Peter Allen and Robert Herman, this path-breaking study was among the first rigorous applications of nonequilibrium thermodynamics to the critical problems faced by contemporary humankind. It appeared in *Goals in a Global Community,* Volume I, the first of two technical volumes that accompanied my more popularly phrased *Goals for Mankind* report to the Club of Rome.

When, after seven years of directing international research programs at the United Nations Institute for Training and Research, I was able to return to my long-standing concerns with evolutionary systems, my contacts with Ilya Prigogine and his school intensified. He, too, has joined the Club of Rome, where debates came increasingly to center on the nature and the governability of complex systems, including human society. During one of my meetings with him, Prigogine asked me to help elaborate the program of the Discoveries 1985 Symposium of the Honda Foundation and the Solvay Institute, as the concern of the organizers coincided with my own interests: it was to clarify the relationship between laws of nature and human conduct. Out of this symposium, held in Brussels in the fall of 1985, came another significant encounter, this time with Jonas Salk. Our latest thinking, to my (and I think also to his) delight, proved to have developed along very similar paths. We both recognized the societal applicability of evolutionary concepts and were conscious of the urgent need to bring together a critical mass of "evolvers" who might inject, in Salk's words, a timely vaccine in the social organism, enabling it to respond positively to the challenges of a rapid transformation. I was soon able to assemble a small group of scientists with a wide variety of backgrounds, and Salk promptly invited this group to meet with him at the Salk Institute. It was as a follow-up to this meeting, which took place in La Jolla in February 1986, that the General Evolution Research Group came into being.

The interaction of the members of the Research Group proved to have an unexpectedly rapid catalytic effect: two volumes of essays written by members of the group were completed within six months; another meeting, this time with public lectures, was held in Florence in October 1986 in celebration of that city as cultural capital of Europe; two monographs and six individually authored books, to be published under a joint aegis, are going to press as I write these Acknowledgments; and *World Futures,* a global problems–oriented publication for which I have long served as editor, was reoriented and became the quarterly journal of the group.

The manuscript of the present volume, in preparation since 1984, was read and discussed by Ilya Prigogine and Jonas Salk, as well as the members of the General Evolution Research Group. I would like to use this opportunity to express my gratitude for their interest, their wisdom, and their time. They have added much that is valid and valuable in this work; I alone bear responsibility for shortcomings and mistakes. Having already noted my debt to Ludwig von Bertalanffy and Erich Jantsch, both tragically deceased, and to Ilya Prigogine and Jonas Salk, let me conclude by naming the founding members of the group individually. They are mathematician Ralph Abraham of the University of California at Santa Cruz; historian Robert Artigiani of the U.S. Naval Academy at Annapolis, Maryland; philosophers Gianluca Bocchi and Mauro Ceruti of the University of Geneva, Switzerland; astrophysicist Eric Chaisson of Harvard University and MIT in Cambridge, Massachusetts; biologist Vilmos Csányi of the Oetvös Lóránd University; Budapest, Hungary; social historian and feminist Riane Eisler of the Institute for Futures Forecasting at Carmel, California; social psychologist and futures forecaster David Loye, likewise of the Institute at Carmel; and biological psychologist Jonathan Schull of Haverford College, Haverford, Pennsylvania. Last but not least, it is my pleasant and proud duty to thank my son Alexander Laszlo, graduate student in systems science and in history and sociology of science at the University of Pennsylvania for the many careful readings of successive rewrites of the manuscript, for his suggestions for further readings, and for the many hours and indeed nights spent in serious discussion.

EVOLUTION
The Grand Synthesis

Introduction

A reader opening a book with the title *Evolution: The Grand Synthesis* may wonder: Why should I concern myself with evolution? And just what precisely is a "grand synthesis"?

It is as well to answer these questions right at the outset. Evolution, as the reader well knows (unless of course he or she is a stout creationist) is the process that brings into being the many biological species that surround us and indeed include us. But evolution is not limited to biological species: if other things in the cosmos were not created as they are but came into being in the course of time they, too, must have evolved. Physical scientists claim that all the furniture of the universe—stars, galaxies, interstellar matter, even space and time as we know them—came into being in a vast process called cosmic evolution. And social scientists tell us that modern societies likewise developed from earlier, less complex forms of organization among human beings.

Our species, the cosmos, modern society—all these *evolved* into what they are today. Are these "evolutions" entirely separate, or are they somehow related?

Modern scientists like to tend their own gardens and do not often look across into the plots of neighboring disciplines. Physical scientists mind cosmic evolution, life scientists mind biological evolution, and social scientists mind historical development, the evolution of human societies. Of course, it has occurred even to the most specialized scientists that their field may be connected in some way to neighboring fields. This possibility can hardly be ignored today, especially as an entire array of "hyphenated" disciplines has sprung up at the interface between the different realms of scientific investigation. The best known and perhaps most significant among them are bio-physics at the interface be-

3

tween physics and biology, and socio-biology at the interface between biology and the social sciences. The results achieved in these fields, even if occasionally controversial, furnish adequate proof that the physical, the biological, and the social realms in which evolution unfolds are by no means disconnected. At the very least, one kind of evolution prepares the ground for the next. Out of the conditions created by evolution in the physical realm emerge the conditions that permit biological evolution to take off. And out of the conditions created by biological evolution come the conditions that allow human beings—and many other species—to evolve certain social forms of organization.

To the reader who believes that science can tell us something of interest about reality, all this is rather obvious. But the reader may still wonder why evolution, unitary or disparate, should be of immediate concern to him or her. After all, it may be that the origin of a thing has little to do with the way it exists once it has evolved. To claim the contrary is to reduce human beings to protozoa, modern society to the hunting-gathering tribe, and the contemporary universe to the quark and the photon.

The point is well taken, except that it disregards the fact that evolution is a continuing process. Nothing that has ever emerged in this world—and that manages to persist in it—is exempt from further evolution. There is no atom of hydrogen in the vast reaches of space and time that would not be subject to transmutation into helium if it encountered the required pressures and temperatures. There is no species on earth that would be safe from mutation, or extinction. If human beings no longer seem to evolve as a biological species, they certainly do evolve as members of human society: the leading edge of human evolution is no longer genetic, it is sociocultural. The future of any thing or being now in existence is not uniquely determined by its past—its evolution. It is determined, rather, by its present—but that, too, is evolution. Evolution is the maker of the future: at each step along the way it writes the scenario of its own continued unfolding.

The future is decided in the interaction between the thing or being that evolves and its environment. Because the environment is never the same for very long, each thing and being is constantly subject to surprises. And because in the last analysis the environment is made up of other things and beings, each atom, each amoeba, and each human being constantly enters into the evolution of all the others. Of course, there are degrees of relevance. The energy released by the splitting of a hydrogen atom in my vicinity enters more strongly into my evolution than the transmutation of a hydrogen atom in the outer reaches of the Andromeda Galaxy. (Indeed, if the former is part of an uncontrolled chain reaction, my evolution may come to a premature end.) Yet, even if qualified with different degrees of immediacy and relevance, the old adage "everything is connected with everything else" describes a true state of affairs.

It follows, then, that to grasp what is fundamental about the evolution of each thing in the universe, we should know something about the evolution of all things. This is clearly impracticable. But we *can* know something about the general patterns of change and development that occur and recur in specific realms. The search for such general patterns can focus attention on truly basic features and help us avoid being trapped or sidetracked by marginally relevant detail.

Philosophers and philosophizing scientists have often searched for general patterns of change and development and many have claimed to have found them. But classical theories rested on sketchy evidence, complemented by generous doses of speculation and personal insight. Today the situation is different. Scientific evidence of the patterns traced by evolution in the physical universe, in the living world, and even in the world of history is growing rapidly. It is coalescing into the image of basic regularities that repeat and recur. It is now possible to search out these regularities and obtain a glimpse of the fundamental nature of evolution—of the evolution of the cosmos as a whole, including the living world and the world of human social history.

To search out and systematically state these regularities is to engage in the creation of the "grand synthesis" that unites physical, biological, and social evolution into a consistent framework with its own laws and logic.

Such a grand evolutionary synthesis is supremely relevant to our own life and times. Ours has been called an age of uncertainty and transformation. It is an age in which contemporary societies are exposed to profound stresses and are undergoing rapid and often unforeseen change. But it is also an age of opportunity. We can now begin to make sense of the confusing tangle of facts and events that make up the history of human societies and understand the most basic laws of change and transformation. A grand evolutionary synthesis can give us the large-scale map that shows us where we are in nature's scheme and that, like any good map, can allow us to identify the processes that concern us the most—those processes that decide the future of our societies, and thus of ourselves.

In the pages that follow, I have been able to give only a preliminary sketch of the main elements of such a grand synthesis. But this first effort will soon be followed by others, researched and written by a new breed of scientist: the multidisciplinary evolutionary thinker who specializes in being a generalist in the study and synthesis of the fields and realms of evolution. The vistas that open today to the specialized evolutionary generalist are vast, and far more profound and exciting than those of the narrowly compartmentalized specialist. The times when scientists could distrust theories in direct proportion to their breadth and dismiss integrative research as "metaphysics" are past. The age of analysis has done its work; the age of synthesis has begun. A synthesis based on the new concepts and theories of evolution has scientific validity as well as pragmatic significance. It helps us clarify our place and role in the scheme of things, and creates that uneliminable minimum of knowledge that is the necessary condition of life and well-being in a complex and changing world. Few endeavors could match it in intellectual excitement and in practical import.

Part One

The Logic of Evolution

1

The Rise of the Evolutionary Paradigm

Systems scientific and philosophic, said Alfred North Whitehead, come and go. Each method of limited understanding is at length exhausted. In its prime each system is a triumphant success: in its decay it is an obstructive nuisance. Whitehead's dictum is true of the systems and methods of the contemporary sciences. The triumphant success of the Newtonian system became an obstructive nuisance at the beginning of the century when Einstein's theory fought for acceptance, Darwin's synthetic theory remained an obstruction in the way of the newer, more adequate theories of species evolution in the 1970s, and the positivistic conception of history remains an obstacle in the way of sustained attempts to inquire into patterns in the evolution of human societies still today.

But a new system, scientific in origin and philosophic in depth and scope, is now on the rise. It goes beyond the limited understanding conveyed by theories within delimited fields of inquiry. It encompasses the great realms of the material universe, of the world of the living, and of the world of history. This is the evolutionary paradigm: the framework for studying the adventure of open systems as they pursue their careers in spheres of nature ever further removed from the inert state of thermodynamic equilibrium, ever more complex and dynamic, ever more in control of themselves and of their environment.

The advent of the new paradigm is a major step in the advance of contemporary science. Science may not be provable, but, as Sir Karl Popper said, it is improvable. The new evolutionary paradigm is an improvement over the previous, discipline-bound theories and paradigms, for it explains more with less. Its basic assumptions and fundamental theorems remain unchanged as we pass from the realm of matter to the sphere of life, and from the sphere of life to the domain of history. Its simplicity and scope are consistent with enduring values that define the course of scientific progress. Simplicity, "elegance," extensibility, consistency, and scope of applicability have always motivated the efforts of scientists; they came clearly to be expressed in the works of Copernicus and Newton, Einstein and Heisenberg. Today they find expression in what has sometimes been called the "evolutionary vision"—the basic set of concepts that defines the interdisciplinary paradigm of system change, persistence, and transformation in the world at large.

The evolutionary paradigm is emerging in field after field; its validity is acknowledged by more and more scientists. They recognize that the new paradigm can suggest concrete ways and means to solve many of the puzzles in their own special yet subtly interconnected discipline. The new paradigm marks the coming of a new era in scientific thinking: an era in which evolution, expressed in human beings and in human societies, is becoming conscious of itself.

ANTECEDENTS OF THE NEW PARADIGM

The new paradigm of evolution did not emerge, like Venus from the sea, all at once, fully created and perfect in every detail. Fundamentally similar ideas have inspired many of the great intellectual currents of human civilization, from Taoism in the East to the Ionian natural philosophers in the West. But these ideas were based on speculation and insight rather than scientific data and tested hypothesis. It is only in our own day that the evolutionary paradigm could reappear within the more tested and hence more reliable framework of science itself.

Without pretending to offer anything like an exhaustive historical account, we can sample some features of Western intellectual history to trace the fortunes of synthesizing evolutionary thinking and its recent entry within science proper. We begin with the ancient Greeks, the first to examine the myths of creation in the cool light of reason.

Almost three thousand years ago, the Ionian natural philosophers began to create a grand evolutionary synthesis that would explain the origin and nature of all things through basic and mutually consistent concepts. They were struck by the diversity of the things encountered in experience and applied themselves to showing how it could have come about from common origins.

In the sixth century before Christ, Thales taught that all things in the world originate from a common source, which he identified as water. His contemporary Anaximander did not regard water as the sole substance from which all others arise. He did not identify the precise nature of the original substance although he did say that it was unfamiliar and limitless and encompassed all the worlds. Earth, fire and water were constantly transforming according to an ordering principle based on justice. Anaximenes, a student of Anaximander, speculated that the primeval substance was a mixture of water and earth. Warmed by the sun, the mixture generated plants, animals, and human beings by spontaneous creation. Air, being of even greater importance than either water or earth, produced all substances through condensation. Fire was but rarefied air that, when condensed, became cloud, water, earth, and ultimately stone.

Among the classical Greeks the wish to be consistent led to further syntheses, of a more or less evolutionary character. Heraclites, who thought fire the most important of the substances, placed stress on eternal becoming: on the principle that "change is all." One cannot step into the same river twice; one cannot identify anything in the world for what it truly is; it is constantly changing. Empedocles, in turn, viewed all things as composed of air, earth, fire, and water in measures determined by the principle of love, which binds, and of hate, which separates. From fires within the earth arose the primal forms that later evolved into the familiar organisms. Many were imperfect and disappeared, while those that proved perfect survived.

With Socrates the naturalism of the pre-Socratics became tuned to the human world: man is the measure. Plato maintained a systematic view of the whole of reality, if only as a "likely tale": he believed all things in the perceived world to be images or shadows of eternal and unchanging Forms or Ideas. Aristotle replaced this conception with a new, more careful naturalism based in part on observation integrated in a truly encyclopedic range of knowledge. His "great chain of being" extended from inanimate objects through plants and animals to humans. The progressive development of nature was matched by a ripening of the soul. The inorganic became the organic through metamorphosis, and in the realm of the organic, animals with powers of sensibility were more animate than plants, endowed merely with the powers of nourishment and sensibility. Nature proceeded gradually and constantly from the least to the most perfect, becoming ever more complex in the process. Nothing, Aristotle said, exists without a cause; the progression is not accidental: it is motivated by a final cause, and this is perfection.

Without revering the Greek philosophers as much as Whitehead, who claimed that all Western philosophy is but a series of footnotes to Plato, or following in the footsteps of the scholastics, whose aim was mainly to reconcile the Christian doctrine with the teachings of Aristotle, we can nevertheless skip over the intellectual history of the period between the late Hellenic and the modern Renaissance: although it includes Epicurus and Lucretius as well as Augustine and Thomas Aquinas, it did not contribute much to the advancement of an embracing evolutionary paradigm. A new beginning was made only with the emancipation of science from church dogma in the Renaissance of the fifteenth century. This was truly a beginning, a restatement of the most elementary observations in a language devoid of reliance on either Aristotle or on theology. But with exceptional geniuses like Leonardo even minute observations ranged over enormous terrain, from marine fossils to shadows on the moon. Copernicus, however, was already a scientific specialist, though with a deep belief in rational principles such as "Nature loves simplicity." His quest to understand celestial mechanics through the simplest possible system of explanations led to the heliocentric hypothesis, reviving and substantiating an idea already known to the ancient Greeks. Galileo, experimenting with inclined planes and falling objects, advanced the concept of a law of gravitation, while Kepler, equipped with the telescope and with an analytical mind, removed the vestiges of mythical rationalism from Copernican theories by showing that the planets described ellipses, and not perfect (and perfectly simple) circles around the sun. Newton, producing perhaps the greatest synthesis of all times, laid the foundations for modern physics by uniting the terrestrial with the celestial sphere through the universal law of gravitation and the equally universal laws of motion.

The emancipation of science led to stress on experiment instead of dogma, and experiment, given the primitive means and instruments available, privileged problems that could be solved with basic formulas of universal application. With Newtonian physics the physical universe became a uniform mechanism which, once wound up, churned out harmonious motions for all eternity. The world view of modern science became mechanistic and soulless, in full contradiction with the world of the living. With the splitting of the known world into a mechanistic universe and a separate realm of life and mind, attempts to create an embracing science of evolution and development encountered an obstacle as formidable as Christian theology. Natural philosophy became divorced from moral philosophy, physics from biology, and the natural sciences from the human and social disciplines.

With Descartes the separation of the realms of matter and mind achieved the status of metaphysical doctrine. The physical universe, including the bodies of living organisms, was but a mechanism, describable by a small number of God-given physical laws. Human mind and consciousness were removed from this sphere and became a separate substance, existing not in space but only in time. Seeking to overcome dualism in his naturalist ethics, Spinoza embraced pantheism, identifying nature with God. Kant, who in his early work on universal natural history asserted that all observable phenomena have natural causes, and who attempted to trace the development of higher forms of life to elementary designs, succumbed in his influential *Critiques* to the posture that separated the knower from the known, and made the natural world into an unattainable "noumenon."

Not until the puzzle of the two and opposing arrows of time was resolved in the late twentieth century was there a sound basis for bridging the gap between matter and mind, the natural world and the human world, and thus between the "two cultures" of modern Western civilization.

THE PUZZLE OF TWO ARROWS OF TIME

Although by the early eighth century scientists tended to view the world as the result of changes that took place in its past, science was stymied throughout the nineteenth century by the persistent contradiction between a mechanistic world slated to run down and an organic world seeming to wind up. With respect to the latter, creationism proved to be a temporary expedient with its claim that species did not evolve (and hence the living world did not really progress in a direction contrary to physical nature)—they were special creations of a supreme mind. Linnaeus, who founded the modern system of classification in botany and biology, said that "there are as many species as originally created by the Infinite End." Organisms, in the view of many biologists, did not reproduce: they "engendered." Generation was the result of the creative act which logically called for God, the great craftsman. Physicists could say nothing about life and its origins and evolution: Newton bracketed out the irreversible changes that lie at the root of all evolutionary processes. The laws of classical mechanics apply regardless of whether a process or particle proceeds from point A to point B or from point B to point A. As particles move in time as well as in space, in Newtonian physics time and motion are fully reversible.

By the middle of the nineteenth century both the physical and the life sciences found themselves enmeshed in endless contradictions concerning the nature of change. Among the physical sciences classical thermodynamics dealt with one-way processes in nature and admitted the irreversibility of time. In the life sciences Darwin's theories of the origin of species, based on one-way processes of cumulative change in the world of the living, created a veritable revolution. The evolutionary processes postulated in classical thermodynamics and Darwinian biology conflicted with classical physics; they also conflicted with each other. The one-way processes discovered by classical thermodynamics and Darwinian biology did not match. In classical thermodynamics the "arrow of time" points downward, toward states of disorganization and randomness, while in Darwinian biology it points upward, toward higher levels of organization in determinate structures and functions. Since Newton's classical mechanics was not challenged until the beginning of the present century, nineteenth-century natural science found itself saddled with two arrows of time—and a framework of classical physics that knew nothing of either.

The imagination of philosophers and social scientists was captured first and foremost by the upward sweep of time in the Darwinian theory. Building on the concepts of German biologists and greatly encouraged by the publication of *The Origin of Species,* the English philosopher Herbert Spencer published his *First Principles*—a comprehensive, science-based account of evolution as leading to the greatest perfection and the most perfect happiness. Likewise impressed by Darwin, Marx and Engels followed the upward sweep of Hegel's evolutionary optimism in their encompassing theory of evolution in nature and in society, known as dialectical and historical materialism.

These were among the noteworthy attempts of nineteenth-century philosophers and scientists to formulate a grand evolutionary synthesis based on the findings of modern science. But in today's hindsight, their efforts were premature. The puzzle of the two arrows of time could not be resolved within nineteenth-century science, and grand syntheses based on such science had to opt between the downward-pointing arrow of thermodynamics and the upward-oriented arrow of biology. Spencer and Marx, among others, opted for the upward sweep of Darwin and ignored the persistent degrading effect of time in classical thermodynamics.

Classical thermodynamics, however, could not be ignored for long. Its basic concepts were formulated by Sadi Carnot in 1824 and elaborated by William Thompson in his 1852 treatise "on the universal tendency in nature to the dissipation of mechanical energy." In 1865 Rudolf Clausius introduced the quantitative definition of entropy—the measure of organization versus randomness in a system—and in 1872 Boltzman advanced the formulation that linked thermodynamics with statistical mechanics and established the discipline as a major field in physical science.

The famous Second Law of Thermodynamics affirmed that for any given system conceived as a closed—in fact, an isolated—unit of matter and energy, differences and gradients in concentration and temperature tend to disappear, to be replaced by uniformity and randomness. The universe, at least its material components, moves from a more organized and energetic state toward states of growing homogeneity and randomness. It ultimately reaches the state of perfect heat distribution in which no irreversible processes can any longer occur: there are no hotter and colder bodies to create a flow of energy. The arrow of time is thus given by the probability that closed systems run down, that they move *toward* equilibrium rather than *away* from it.

Although some nineteenth-century philosophers and social scientists ignored it, the conflict between physics and the life sciences became more and more evident. Some of the greatest minds of the epoch began to be preoccupied by it. Of the many ingenious suggestions for resolving it, two deserve special mention. One was made by the French philosopher Henri Bergson. The universe, said Bergson, shows two tendencies: there is a "reality which is making itself in a reality which is unmaking itself." The general tendency to repetition and the dissipation of energy, discovered by thermodynamics, is the tendency of "matter"; the countertendency within it, documented by Darwin, is the tendency of "life." The evolution of life is the result of the workings of a basic impulse called the *élan vital*. It thrusts itself forward into ever-new forms of organized structure. These structures store and utilize energy and maintain their capacity for growth and adaptation up to a point; then they lapse into repetitive routine and ultimately degrade their vital energy.

Another noteworthy suggestion was put forward by Ludwig Boltzman, one of the founders of classical thermodynamics. Conceive of the current state of the universe, he said, as but a brief deviation from equilibrium. Our world is only one of several regions which are in disequilibrium; among these worlds the probabilities of their state (i.e., their entropy) increase as often as they decrease. In the universe as a whole the two directions of time are indistinguishable, so that a living organism in one of these regions can always define the direction of time as going from the less probable to the more probable state. The former state is its "past" and the latter its "future."

However ingenious, Boltzman's proposal could no more resolve the conflict between the Second Law of Thermodynamics and Darwinian evolution than that of Bergson. Postulating two layers of reality, one called matter and the other life (the latter infused by a mysterious *élan vital*), and making our world into a brief interval balanced by others tending in the opposite direction (with all such locally disbalanced regions having arbitrary definitions of time), makes for speculative cosmology rather than sound science. Scientists had to wait for nonequilibrium thermodynamics and the new cosmology of the 1970s to perceive that there is no need for metaphysical solutions to the conflict between upward-tending biological evolution and the downward-tending processes of closed physical systems.

We have now come to see that the conflict between the two great processes—the two arrows of time—is only apparent. Evolving systems are not closed; the universe as a whole is not mechanistic; cosmic processes do not point the arrow of time toward a state of universal heat-death; and life is neither an accidental aberration nor the manifestation of mysterious metaphysical forces.

It took the better part of two millennia for the evolutionary paradigm to reassert itself within the more solid framework of empirical science, and almost two centuries for empirical science to emancipate itself from the dogmas of the Middle Ages. But in our day at last, the evolutionary paradigm surfaces as the dominant mode of thought underlying work in almost all of the natural sciences, and in many of the social sciences as well. Notwithstanding remnants of compartmentalization and pockets of resistance (by scientific specialists as well as dogmatic creationists), evolutionary thinking is here to stay. If integrated within a general yet sound synthesis, its results can add up to a new and more fruitful conception of the nature of reality, in the universe at large as well as here on earth. Those who make creative use of the new conception will be the leading minds of our time, whose vision will open new vistas for science and fresh opportunities for people and societies.

2

Foundations of the Grand Synthesis

In the penultimate decade of the twentieth century science is sufficiently advanced to resolve the puzzles that stymied scientists in the last century and demonstrate, without metaphysical speculation, the consistency of evolution in all realms of experience. It is now possible to advance a grand evolutionary synthesis (GES) based on unitary and mutually consistent concepts derived from the empirical sciences. We can lay the foundation for this major interdisciplinary endeavor by assembling and analyzing the basic concepts of the contemporary sciences of evolution.

The processes and manifestations of evolution are now investigated not only in contemporary variants of classical disciplines, but also in a handful of freshly emerging fields. The new sciences deal with the appearance, development, and functioning of complex systems regardless of the domain of investigation to which they belong. They originated with the general system theory pioneered by Ludwig von Bertalanffy, Paul Weiss, Anatol Rapoport, and Kenneth Boulding, and with the science of cybernetics developed by Norbert Wiener, W. Ross Ashby, and Stafford Beer. Since the 1960s they were joined and reinforced by nonequilibrium thermodynamics, the work of Aharon Katchalsky and Ilya Prigogine and their followers, by cellular automata theory pioneered by John von Neumann and evolved in the autopoietic system theory of Humberto Maturana and Francisco Varela, and by catastrophe theory and dynamic systems theory developed by René Thom, Christopher Zeeman, Robert Shaw, and Ralph Abraham, among others. As these fields of science—known collectively as sciences of complexity—offer the most logical foundation for GES, we now review their pertinent concepts and conceptions. (Readers inter-

ested in technical details should consult the "Notes" section at the
end of this book.)

BASIC CONCEPTS

Equilibrium, Determinism, and Scientific Law

We can best introduce the fundamental concepts of the new
evolutionary sciences by contrasting their basic features with some
received notions of more traditional theories.

The contrast is indeed striking. Traditionally the natural sciences
viewed evolution as a basically deterministic process oriented
toward equilibrium. Factors of chance and instability were under-
emphasized in favor of stability, control, and predictability. While
in physics randomness was conceptualized in quantum mechanics,
it was limited to the realm of the microscopic; at macroscopic
levels phenomena were considered to be basically deterministic.
The mechanistic world view underlying Newtonian physics, and
the Laplacean belief that, given enough information, we could
predict the position of every particle in the universe at any time,
was highly persuasive and long dominant. The laws of nature had
to be deterministic as well as universal; exceptions to them were
viewed with mistrust and ascribed to flaws in the system of
reckoning. The states toward which systems move in many complex but basically deterministic processes were thought to be
states of equilibrium—of relaxed tensions, rest and balance.

Concepts of equilibrium and determinacy were dominant also in
the sciences of life and society. Biologists resorted to the deterministic logic whereby natural selection brings about a proper balance between predator and prey and assures the survival of the
fittest under predictable conditions. Economists, following in the
footsteps of Adam Smith, are still loath to surrender the central
place of equilibrium in their theories (Kenneth Boulding may have
been right when he remarked of modern economics that "nothing
fails like success"): general equilibrium theory is not, as yet, an
expression of the evolutionary paradigm. Neither is the typical
theory produced by today's social scientists—in most cases they
study statics instead of dynamics; structures and states instead of

processes and functions; self-correcting mechanisms instead of self-organizing systems; conditions of equilibrium instead of dynamic balances in regions of distinct disequilibrium.

The evolutionary paradigm challenges concepts of equilibrium and determinacy in scientific theories; and it modifies the classical deterministic conception of scientific laws. The laws conceptualized in the evolutionary context are not deterministic and prescriptive: they do not uniquely determine the course of evolution. Rather, they state ensembles of possibilities within which evolutionary processes can unfold. They are rules of the game, to be exploited in each individual instance according to the skills and predispositions of the players. Dynamic systems—the "players" in the game of evolution—are not strictly determined. They do not have individual trajectories (evolutionary paths) but bundles of trajectories. If we consider all their trajectories starting from a particular region, no matter how small, then we find that these trajectories separate after a time into quite different regions. As Nobel-laureate thermodynamicist Ilya Prigogine points out, dynamic systems have a basic "divergence property." This property undermines classical determinism, based on the concept of a single trajectory. Given identical initial conditions, different sequences of events unfold—within the limits and the possibilities set by the laws. The sequences in turn create fresh sets of limits and possibilities. Evolution is always possibility and never destiny. Its course is logical and comprehensible, but it is not predetermined and thus not predictable.

Systems in the Third State

A grand synthesis of the myriad forms and processes of evolution is possible because, as the sciences of complexity now discover, evolution is nevertheless singularly consistent: it brings forth the same basic kind of entity in all its domains. This entity is a system of a particular kind—a system that we may best identify as "system in the third state."

The fact is that systems in the real world can exist in one of three types of states. Of these three, one is radically different from classical conceptions: it is the state far from thermal and chemical equilibrium. The other two states are those in which systems are either *in* equilibrium or *near* it. In a state of equilibrium, energy and matter flows have eliminated differences in temperature and concentration; the elements of the system are unordered in a random mix, and the system itself is homogeneous and dynamically inert. The second state differs only slightly from the first: in systems near equilibrium there are small differences in temperature and concentration; the internal structure is not random and the system is not inert. Such systems will tend to move toward equilibrium as soon as the constraints that keep them in nonequilibrum are removed. For systems of this kind, equilibrium remains the "attractor" which it reaches when the forward and reverse reactions compensate one another statistically, so that there is no longer any overall variation in the concentrations (a result known as the law of mass action, or Guldberg and Waage's law). The elimination of differences between concentrations corresponds to chemical equilibrium, just as uniformity of temperature corresponds to thermal equilibrium. While in a state of nonequilibrium the system performs work and therefore produces entropy, at equilibrium no further work is performed and entropy production ceases.[1]

The third possible state of systems is the state far from thermal and chemical equilibrium. Systems in this state are nonlinear and occasionally indeterminate. They do not tend toward minimum free energy and maximum entropy but may amplify certain fluctuations and evolve toward a new dynamic regime that is radically different from stationary states at or near equilibrium.

Prima facie, the evolution of systems in the third state appears to contradict the Second Law of Thermodynamics. How can systems actually increase their level of complexity and organization, and become more energetic? The Second Law states that in any isolated system organization and structure tend to disappear, to be replaced by uniformity and randomness. But unlike scientists in the nineteenth century, contemporary investigators realize that evolving systems are not isolated systems, and thus the Second Law does not fully describe what takes place in them—more precisely, between them and their environment. The fact we now realize is that systems in the third state are open systems, and the change of entropy within them is not determined uniquely by irreversible processes within their boundaries. Internal processes within the system do obey the Second Law: free energy, once expended, is unavailable to perform further work. But energy available to perform further work can be "imported" by open systems from their environment. There can be a transport of free energy—or negative entropy—across the system boundaries.[2] When the two quantities—the free energy within the system, and the free energy transported across the system boundaries from the environment—balance and offset each other, the system is in a steady (i.e., stationary) state. But in a dynamic environment the two terms seldom precisely balance over any extended period of time; therefore, the systems that evolve in the real world tend to fluctuate around certain states that define their dynamic steady states, rather than settle into them without variation.

The matter-energy systems that emerge in the course of evolutionary processes in the real world are systems in the third state, far from thermal and chemical equilibrium. Such systems evolve in the universe as in the course of time matter decouples from radiation and, in its uneven distribution in galaxies and stars, creates intense and enduring energy flows. (For details see the processes of cosmic evolution described in Chapter 3.)

The Continuum of Evolution

The processes of evolution unfold in all domains of the empirical world: in the physical universe the same as in the world of the living. They produce systems in the third state—dynamic matter-energy systems far from equilibrium. These systems form a continuum that bridges the traditional boundaries of classical disciplines. This becomes evident if we compare systems that have emerged in the course of time in the universe and on earth in regard to some basic parameters. The relevant parameters include size, organizational level, bonding energy, and level of complexity.

Concentrating first on size, organizational level, and bonding energy, we find a truly elegant continuum. As we move from microscopic systems on a basic level of organization to macroscopic systems on higher organizational levels, we move from systems that are strongly and rigidly bonded to those with weaker and more flexible binding energies. Relatively small units with strong binding forces act as building blocks in the formation of

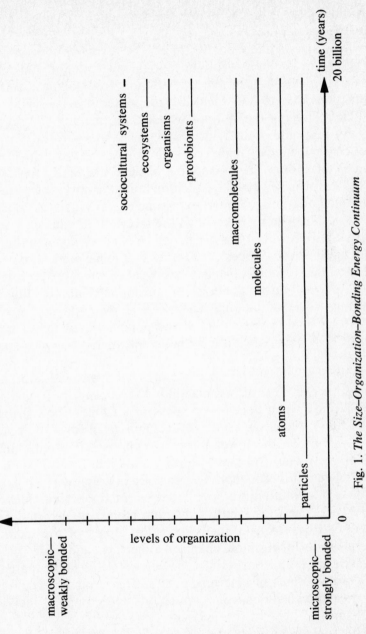

Fig. 1. *The Size–Organization–Bonding Energy Continuum*

larger and less strongly bound systems on higher levels of organization. These in turn become building blocks in still larger, higher-level, and less strongly bonded units.

The continuum of size, organizational level, and bonding energy appears throughout the range of evolution, from the basic particles of the universe to the highest-level systems of the biosphere. Particles such as the quark—whether or not any of them can actually be found as individual units in nature—are known to be bound by enormously high forces. Protons and neutrons within the nucleus of atoms are bound by nuclear exchange forces, the strength of which is strikingly demonstrated in nuclear fission. The outer shell of atoms is bound to the nucleus by electronic bonding, an entire dimension weaker than the forces of the nucleus. Atoms within complex molecules are joined by ionic or covalent bonding and related weaker forces. The forces that join chemical molecules within organic macromolecules are weaker still, while those that bond cells within multicellular organisms are another dimension down the scale of bonding energy. Whatever the nature of the bonds that bind organic species and populations within ecologies and social systems, they are yet more ephemeral than physical and biochemical bonds.

Proportionately to the decrease of binding energies we find an increase in the level of organization. The concept of organization level is understood here in the sense of a Chinese-box structural hierarchy of "boxes within boxes." On a given level of organization, systems on the lower level function as subsystems; on the next higher level of organization, systems jointly form suprasystems. Using this concept, we can readily appreciate that the products of evolution are distributed on multiple hierarchical levels. Several particles jointly constitute atomic nuclei, and nuclei surrounded by electron shells form the atoms of the elements. Several atoms form simple chemical molecules, and more complex polymers are built from simpler molecules. Cells, in turn, are built from various kinds of macromolecules, organisms from cells, and ecologies and societies from populations and groups of individual organisms.

Evolution's level of organization does not determine the structural complexity of a system—the higher level is not necessarily more complex than its subsystems. For example, the structure of a molecule such as H₂O is considerably simpler than the atomic structure of hydrogen and oxygen. The structure of a cell colony is simpler than the structure of the constituent cells, and the structure of a termite colony, a baboon society, or an ecology is simpler than the organic structure of their individual members.[3]

There is no contradiction in the affirmation that the higher-level (supra)system is structurally simpler than the lower-level (sub)systems that are its parts. The hierarchy created by the evolution of systems is not only a structural hierarchy but also a *control* hierarchy. In a control hierarchy the suprasystems control certain aspects of the behavior of the subsystems. Less complex systems on a higher level of organization can effectively control more complex systems on lower levels in virtue of the selective disregard, on the higher, controlling level, of the detailed dynamics of the lower-level units. As biophysicist Howard Pattee points out, the selective neglect of irrelevant details is a universal property of hierarchical control systems. Hierarchical controls always arise from internal constraints that force the lower-level units into a pattern of collective behavior that is independent of the details of their dynamic behavior. The emergence of a higher-level system is not a complexification but a *simplification* of system function.

However, once a new hierarchical level has emerged, systems on the new level tend to become progressively more complex. For example, on the atomic level of organization, hydrogen, the first element to be synthesized in the processes of cosmic evolution, is structurally simpler than the subsequently synthesized, heavier elements. On a higher level of organization, a molecule of water is simpler than a protein molecule; on a still higher organizational level, a unicellular organism is less complex than a multicellular one and, on the even higher, *social* level of organization, a colony of baboons is less complex than a human society. Thus, while a new level of organization means a simplification of system function, and of the corresponding system structure, it also means the initiation of a process of progressive structural and functional complexification.

Systems on a higher level of organization include the subsystems on subsidiary organizational levels. Thus the total structure of the higher-level suprasystem is more complex than any of its subsystems. This does not contradict the affirmation that the structure of

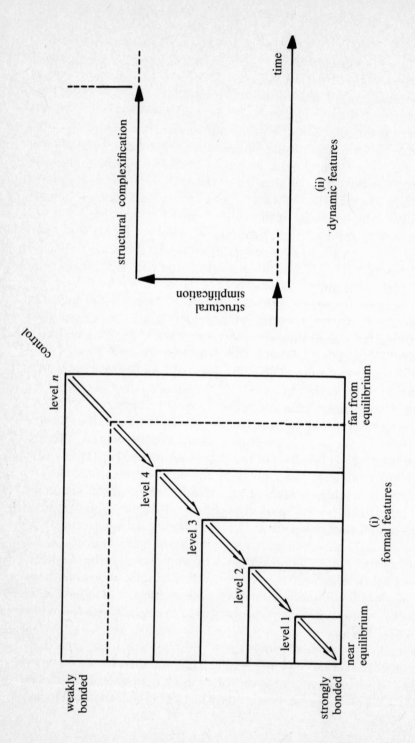

Fig. 1A. *Main Features of the Evolutionary Continuum*

the suprasystem, qua system on its own, defining organizational level, is simpler than the structure of its individual subsystems. A colony of baboons, for example, is structurally simpler by far than the genotype and the phenotype of the individual baboons that are its members. Yet the colony taken as an inclusive total system consists of all the individual baboons, and all the cells, molecules, and atoms in their bodies, plus all the relations that exist between the baboons. Thus, while the colony per se is structurally and functionally simpler than individual baboons, taken as an inclusive total system it is more complex. (Henceforth, when speaking of the structure and function of a system, I shall mean by it the structure and the function of the system on its own organizational level, rather than the total system that includes the structures and the functions of all its subsystems.)

A higher level of organization offers fresh possibilities for complexification; the greater variety of components available to the suprasystem allows a larger range of structural and functional variation, with new connections imposed among the connected subsystems. Thus, by moving to a new organizational level, evolution penetrates to ever higher and more varied forms of structure and function.

The logic of evolution in regard to the formal aspect of its products is simple and elegant: it takes the most basic and strongly bound systems, exposes them to each other, and creates higher-level systems based on the weaker forces that attract the more strongly bound components. The process begins with hadrons, leptons, and quarks; continues with atoms, molecules and cells; and it extends under suitable conditions (such as those on earth) all the way to organisms, ecologies, and societies.

The above are the most fundamental concepts of a grand synthesis of the findings of the new sciences of evolution and complexity. These and related concepts and hypotheses are tested and elaborated in a number of scientific fields and in a variety of ways. Research programs directly concerned with evolution can be roughly divided into two categories: programs that rely on observation and experimentation, and those that construct formal—mathematical and topological—models of system behavior. The empirical and the theoretical approaches complement each other;

both have come up with important results that further specify and develop the basic concepts.

EMPIRICAL FINDINGS

Structure and Free Energy

The evolution of systems in the third state can be empirically observed and tested. It is known that, under suitable conditions, a constant and rich energy flow passing through a system drives it toward states characterized by a higher level of free energy and a lower level of entropy. The relationship between nonequilibrium and self-organization was pointed out by Prigogine as early as 1945. Then, experiments reported by Morowitz in 1968 demonstrated that a flow of energy passing through a nonequilibrium system organizes its structures and components to access, use, and store more and more free energy.[4] The explanation of this phenomenon in thermodynamic terms was given by Aharon Katchalsky in 1971: he showed that increasing energy penetration drives systems consisting of a large number of diffusely coupled nonlinear elements into nonequilibrium.

But the important measure in evolution is not simply energy, nor even free-energy, but free energy flux density. What counts is how much of the free-energy flux density available in the environment is captured, retained, and used in a system. Free-energy flux density is a measure of the free energy per unit of time per unit of mass: for example, erg/second/gram. A complex chemical system retains more of this factor than a monatomic gas; a living system retains more than a complex chemical system. This indicates a basic direction in evolution, an overarching sweep that, together with the decrease of entropy and of equilibrium, defines the arrow of time in the physical as well as in the biological and the social world.

The relationship between energy flow over time and change in entropy and free energy is essential for answering not only the question as to *how* systems in the third state evolve, but also whether they evolve *necessarily*, under certain conditions. Until the 1970s investigators leaned to the view—exposed most eloquently by Jacques Monod—that evolution is due mainly to accidental factors. But as of the 1980s many scientists are becoming convinced that evolution is not an accident, but occurs necessarily whenever certain parametric conditions are fulfilled.

Laboratory experiments and quantitative formulations now corroborate the nonaccidental character of the processes of evolution. The experiments call for reproducing an energy flow from a source to a sink, and placing the test objects within the flow. As Prigogine points out, the best known experiment of this kind is that which demonstrates the appearance of the so-called Bénard cells.

The experiment is basically simple. A vertical temperature gradient is created in a liquid by heating its lower surface. Thereby a continuous heat flux moves from the bottom toward the top. When the gradient reaches a critical value the state of the liquid in which heat is conveyed upward by conduction becomes unstable. A convection flow is created, increasing the rate of heat transfer. The flow is in the form of a complex spatial organization of molecules in the liquid: moving coherently, they form hexagonal cells of a specific size. The Bénard cells maintain themselves in the heat flow and they dissipate entropy at a high rate. The phenomenon is radically different from the linear processes that occur in systems near equilibrium.

Bénard cells are not limited to laboratory experiments; they occur in nature in a wide variety of circumstances. Wherever there is a complex flow in a medium, forms of new order arise spontaneously. This is true of the flow of heat from the center of a star such as the sun to its outer layers, as well as the flow of warm air from the surface of the earth toward outer space. The earth, warmed by the sun, heats the air from below while outer space, much colder, absorbs heat from the top layers of the atmosphere. As the lower layer of the atmosphere rises and the upper layer drops, circulation vortices are created, and these take the shape of Bénard cells. Closely packed hexagonal lattices, such cells leave their imprint on the pattern of sand dunes in the desert and on the pattern of snowfields in the Arctic. Surrounding us in the many complex flows of the biosphere, Bénard cells are evidence of systemic self-organization in nature: they represent the kind of order encountered in all third-state systems far from thermodynamic equilibrium, whether living or nonliving.

Basic experiments in inorganic chemistry shed light on how

systems of interacting elements move from states at or near
equilibrium to the domains of nonequilibrium that characterize
systems in the third state. Under controlled laboratory conditions
sets of chemical reactions can be forced to move progressively
further from chemical equilibrium. Near chemical equilibrium the
reaction system is successfully described by solving the chemical
kinetic equations that apply at equilibrium as well as those that
correspond to the Brownian motion of the molecules and the
random mixing of the components. But as reaction rates are
increased, at some point the system becomes unstable and new
solutions are required to explain its state, branching off from those
that apply near equilibrium. The modified solutions signify new
states of organization in the system of reactants: stationary or
dynamic patterns of structure, or chemical clocks of various
frequency. Where the equilibrium branch of the solution becomes
unstable the reaction system acquires characteristics typical of
nonequilibrium systems in general: coherent behavior appears, and
a higher level of autonomy vis-à-vis the environment. The elements cohere into an identifiable unity with a characteristic spatial
and temporal order; there is now a dynamic system, whereas near
equilibrium there were but sets of reactants.

The origins of life on earth may be due to just such a process of
progressive organization in systems of continuous energy flow. It
has been known for some time that steady irradiation by energy
from the sun was instrumental in catalyzing the basic reactions
which led to the first protobionts in shallow primeval seas. A new
hypothesis now suggests that the energy of the earth itself may
have played an essential role, in the form of hot submarine springs
in the Archaean oceans. The hypothesis is significant in that it
requires a series of small continuous flow reactors for the emergence of life, similar in all essential respects to the chemical
reaction systems responsible for Bénard cells as well as for more
complex chemical structures under controlled laboratory conditions. Nature's reaction systems may have consisted of cracking
fronts in the submarine rock which caused sea water to heat
rapidly and to react with chemicals in the rock and in the surrounding sea water. As the hot fluid rose toward the surface it dissipated
its heat. In the continuous flux of energy created by magma
erupting into the sea bottom and interacting with the energy of the
sun in shallow seas and then dissipating into air and water, the

chemicals that served as the basic building blocks of life were constantly mixed. Out of these series of reactions came the proto-bionts—the lipid vesicles from which more complex forms of life have evolved in time.

Systems with significant unity, autonomy, and ordered structure and behavior emerge when sets of reactants are exposed to an energy flow. If there is sufficient diversity in the components and sufficient complexity in their structure, the resulting system will have bistability or multistability—that is, it will be capable of persisting in more than one steady state. In more complex systems there will also be various feedbacks and catalytic cycles among the subsystems or principal components.

In nature, systems in the third state almost always exhibit some variety of catalytic cycles. Such cycles tend to be selected in the course of time in virtue of their remarkable capacity for persist-ence under a wide range of conditions. They have great stability and fast reaction rates. Already in 1931 Lars Onsager could show that in a steady-state system, cyclic matter-energy flows are likely to arise. For example, in a simple chemical system composed of three types of molecules, A, B, and C, in which both forward and reverse reactions are possible (e.g., $A \rightleftharpoons B$, $B \rightleftharpoons C$, $C \rightleftharpoons A$) the introduction of a continuous energy irradiation into one of the cycles, (e.g., $A + hv \rightarrow B$) tends to move the system into a cyclic pattern $(A \rightarrow B \rightarrow C \rightarrow A)$. More recently Manfred Eigen and Peter Schuster have demonstrated that catalytic cycles are the basis for the persistence of the complex structures which underlie, and make possible, the emergence of life.

In relatively simple chemical systems, autocatalytic reactions tend to dominate, while in more complex processes, characteristic of living phenomena, entire chains of cross-catalytic cycles ap-pear.[5] Catalytic cycles underlie the stability of the sequence of nucleic acids that code the structure of living organisms; they also underlie, on a higher organizational level, the persistence of all living forms within the biosphere of our planet.

Convergence to Higher Levels

Given sufficient time, and an enduring energy flow acting on organized systems within permissible parameters of intensity, tem-perature, and concentration, the already evolved catalytic cycles

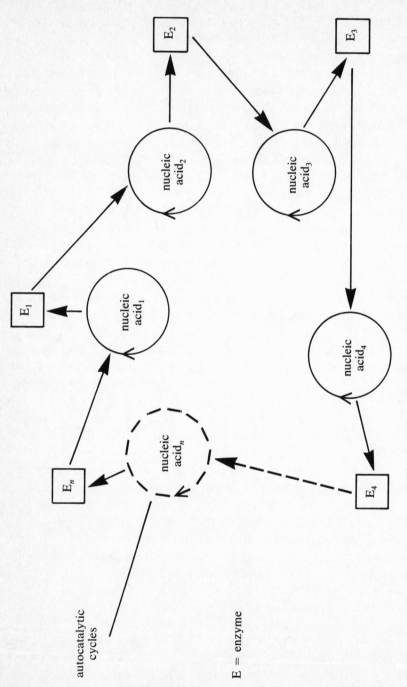

Fig. 2. *A Cross-Catalytic ("Hyper") Cycle*

E = enzyme

autocatalytic
cycles

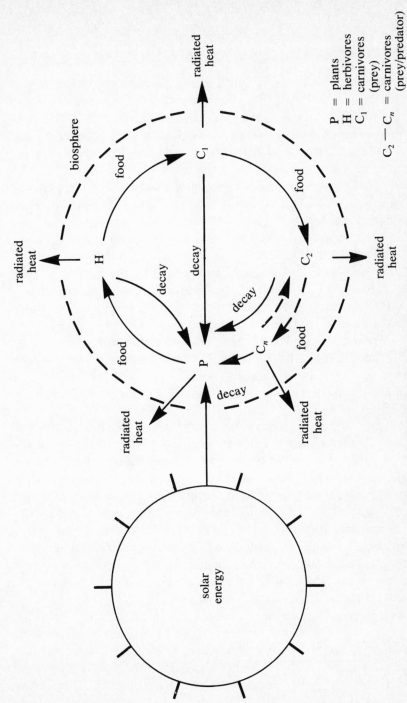

Fig. 3. *Some Major Catalytic Cycles in the Biosphere*

P = plants
H = herbivores
C_1 = carnivores (prey)
$C_2 — C_n$ = carnivores (prey/predator)

tend to interlock in what Eigen calls hypercycles. These are cycles that maintain two or more dynamic systems in a shared environment through coordinated functions, similar to but even more integrated than symbiosis among organic species. For example, on the basic level of living phenomena, nucleic acid molecules carry the information needed to reproduce themselves as well as an enzyme. The enzyme catalyzes the production of another nucleic acid molecule, which in turn reproduces itself plus another enzyme. The loop may involve a large number of elements; ultimately it closes in on itself, forming a cross-catalytic hypercycle remarkable for its fast reaction rates and stability under diverse parametric conditions.

The formation of hypercycles allows dynamic systems to emerge on successively higher levels of organization. On the new level the amount of information that can be handled by the cycle is greater than on lower levels owing to the greater diversity and richness of the components and structures. Evolution thus bypasses the functional optima of complexity that would block further progress on given organizational levels. Instead of drifting randomly around the optimal complexity on level n, the formation of hypercycles allows two or more systems to jointly create a suprasystem on level $n+1$, where fresh structural possibilities offer new horizons for further evolution.

The shift from level to level of organization by means of catalytic hypercycles we can best call *convergence*. (*Hypercycle formation* or *hierarchization* would be correct as well, though these expressions are less clear and clumsier in use.) In this context convergence does not mean growing similarities among systems (as in the convergence of ideologies and socioeconomic systems) since the hypercycle-forming systems functionally complete and complement each other. The outcome of convergence is a higher-level system that selectively disregards many details of the dynamics of its subsystems and imposes an internal constraint that forces the systems into a collective mode of functioning.

Convergence among systems occurs in all realms of evolution. On each level, systems in an energy flow progressively exploit the free-energy fluxes in their environment. As the density of the free energy retained in the systems increases, the systems acquire structural complexity. Because of their convergence, systems on successively higher levels of organization acquire a fresh range of possibilities for setting forth the process by which they retain increasingly dense and abundant free-energy fluxes in structures of growing complexity.

The processes of evolution create systems on multiple hierarchical levels. On each level the structure of the highest system level is initially comparatively simple: simpler than the structure of the component subsystems. (Of course, the complexity of the suprasystem-cum-subsystems is more complex than any of its subsystems: it includes all subsystemic structures plus the relations between them.) The further evolution of the suprasystem then leads to the progressive complexification of its defining system level—and ultimately to the creation of hypercycles that shift it to the next organizational level. Thus evolution moves from the simpler to the more complex type of system, and from the lower to the higher level of organization.[6]

Instability and Transformation

Change occurs and evolution unfolds because dynamic systems in the third state are not entirely stable. They have upper thresholds of stability that, if transgressed, produce critical instabilities. Experiments confirm that dynamic systems far from equilibrium can be moved out of their steady states by changes in some of the environmental parameters. Such systems are critically sensitive to changes in the parameters that are essential for the functioning of the structure-maintaining catalytic cycles. When changes of this kind occur, the systems enter a transitory phase characterized by indeterminacy, randomness, and some degree of chaos, with a relatively high rate of entropy production. The chaotic phase comes to an end when the systems settle into a new dynamic regime. In this new ordered state the systems are again maintained by catalytic cycles and multiple feedbacks, and entropy production drops to a functional minimum.

The way in which systems in the third state respond to destabilizing changes in their environment is of great importance for understanding the dynamics of evolution in all realms of reality. As Part Two will show, there is significant evidence accumulated in many fields of empirical science that dynamic systems do not evolve smoothly and continuously over time, but do so in comparatively sudden leaps and bursts. Third-state systems can evolve through sequences of destabilizations and phases of chaos since they have multiple states of stability: when one steady state is fatally disturbed, other steady-state solutions remain accessible. The further systems are from thermodynamic equilibrium, the more sensitive to change their structure and the more sophisticated the feedbacks and catalytic cycles that maintain it. Complex systems far from equilibrium can exist in many different steady states and the number of possible steady state solutions grows proportionately to their complexity and level of nonequilibrium.

The selection from among the set of dynamically functional alternative steady states is not predetermined. The new state is decided neither by initial conditions in the system nor by changes in the critical values of environmental parameters; when a dynamic system is fundamentally destabilized it acts indeterminately. By an apparently random choice one among its possibly numerous internal fluctuations is amplified, then the fluctuation spreads with great rapidity. The thus "nucleated" fluctuation dominates the system's dynamic regime and determines the nature of its new steady state. Since the number of the available steady states increases proportionately to the level of nonequilibrium, the more dynamic and negentropic the system the greater its degree of freedom in the wake of its destabilization.

Owing to the factor of chance that thus enters the processes of transformation, the evolutionary trajectory of systems in the third state is not predictable in detail. Two systems, even if they start from identical initial conditions and are subject to identical perturbations in the environment, may evolve along divergent trajectories. We cannot predict the precise evolutionary trajectory chosen by any system in the third state; all we can say is that the new steady state, if it is dynamically stable, assimilates the disturbance introduced by the destabilizing parameters within an open structure that is likely to be more dynamic and complex than the structure in the previous steady state.

It is through phases of chance and indeterminacy that evolution tends in the observed general direction of successive levels of organization, with growing dynamism and increasing complexity on each of the organizational levels.

Fig. 4. *Bifurcations: The Increase of Alternatives at Higher Levels*

THEORETICAL FINDINGS

A detailed understanding of the observed dynamics of the evolution of systems in the third state calls for the development of new theoretical tools. This is true in regard to both the self-maintenance of such systems in their environment and the discontinuous, nonlinear nature of their evolution and development.

Autopoiesis

Systems on organizational levels where life emerges are too far from thermodynamic equilibrium to persist indefinitely in their milieu. Such systems can maintain themselves in time only if they evolve the capacity to replicate or reproduce their structure. Using a term introduced by Humberto Maturana in the 1960s, we can describe systems on such relatively high organizational levels as "autopoietic" (from the Greek for "self-creating"). Indeed, cells, organs, organisms, and groups and societies of organisms are autopoietic systems: they renew, repair, and replicate or reproduce themselves. How they do this cannot be known in detail (already a cell consists of some 10^{20} molecules with hundreds of simultaneous reactions), but it can be modeled. Models of autopoiesis are simplified dynamic paraphrases of complex replicative processes in real-world systems.

In the already classic work of Maturana and Francisco Varela, an autopoietic system is defined as a network of interrelated component-producing processes such that the components in interaction generate the same network that produced them. The product is always the network (i.e., the system) itself, created and re-created in a flow of matter and energy. The living cell turns out to be the simplest entity that qualifies as an autopoietic system. It has a catalytic nucleus interacting with an environmental substrate and producing membrane-forming components. The membrane separates the network of interactions that produced it from the rest of the cell. Subcellular structures are defined in the autopoietic model as component-producing components that replicate the network of self-replicating processes.[7] The elements of the model can be computerized, and investigators can simulate the development of various types of self-replicating systems. Since the sub-

strate inputs can be controlled and the rates of membrane formation and disintegration can be regulated, myriad variations can be
induced. Systems with rupture-proof membranes can be produced
with equal facility as systems that are incapable of forming membranes; one variety of systems proves to be self-repairing while
another turns out to have a cancerous growth. Investigators hope
that some of the simulations may prove to be faithful paraphrases
of self-replicating processes not only in cells, but also in organs, in
multicellular organisms, and in ecological and social systems.

Autopoietic modeling evolved from the rigorous mathematical
base of cellular automata theory pioneered by John von Neumann
in the 1960s. Today autopoietic models and cellular automata
theory are in rapid evolution, thanks to ever more powerful
computers. A great variety of self-replicating systems now pursue
their fascinating and often unpredictable developmental cycles in
the electronic workshops of mathematicians. It is often difficult to
say which of these systems simulate real-world systems; a question
rendered even more opaque by the lack of interest many theoreticians profess in the practical application of their models.

Autopoiesis is not evolution, however, even if autopoietic cellular automata models can simulate certain evolutionary phenomena
such as the convergence of cells into multicellular systems. In
order to understand evolution one needs also to understand how
discontinuous, nonlinear change takes place in real-world dynamic
systems. This calls for different types of models, and even for a
new mathematics. (The differential calculus, ordinarily employed
to model change, assumes that change is relatively smooth and
continuous; it becomes almost unmanageably complex when
forced to handle leaps and discontinuities.) It has been dynamic
systems theory that has risen to meet this challenge. The models of
dynamic systems theorists can likewise be computerized, but they
consist not of components with specially designed functions but of
a combination of ordinary differential equations, partial differential
equations of the evolution type, and finite difference equations
singly or in sets.

Catastrophes, Chaos, and Bifurcations

Although the nomenclature of dynamic systems theorists is
decidedly pessimistic, their work is hopeful: it promises to shed

Fig. 5.1. *Orderly Chemical Oscillations* : 1(a) in frequency distribution
1(b) in spatial phase trajectories (e.g., a convergent limit cycle)

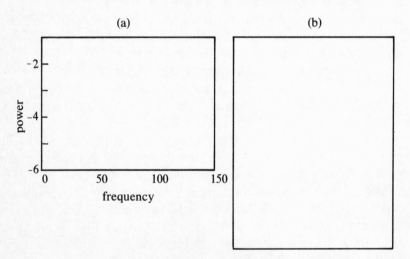

Fig. 5.2. *Chaotic Behavior* : 2(a) in frequency distribution
2(b) in spatial phase trajectories

SOURCE: After I. Prigogine and G. Nicolis, "La chimie de l'aléatoire,"
Chimie Nouvelle 966 (Brussels).

new light on the nonlinear trajectories that characterize the evolution of complex systems in the real world. René Thom, a pioneer of dynamic systems theory, has developed multidimensional topological models that permit a rigorous treatment of the succession of system states even if the pattern of change is fundamental and sudden, that is, if it is "catastrophic"—hence the name "catastrophe theory."[8] Catastrophe theory provides a mathematical tool for the rigorous representation of certain varieties of discontinuous change. However, Thom's standard theory can only model one of a larger variety of radical system changes, namely changes due to the sudden appearance or disappearances of so-called static attractors. Recent work in dynamic systems theory has led to the development of quantitative tools to model catastrophic changes due to the appearance or disappearance of other types of attractors as well, including those known as "periodic" and "chaotic."

In the geometric orientation that dominates in contemporary dynamic systems theory, the principal features of dynamic systems are the attractors: they characterize the long-run behavior of the systems. Dynamic systems evolve from a given initial state along a unique trajectory (or time series) of states in accordance with the laws of evolution. This leads eventually to some recognizable pattern where the trajectory remains trapped. The pattern defines the *attractors* of the system, while the ensemble of the initial states that are attracted by them define their *basin*.

If the series of system states come to a rest, their evolution is governed by a static attractor; if the states consist of a repeated cycle of states with a definite periodicity, the system is under the sway of a periodic attractor. And if the trajectory of system states neither comes to rest nor exhibits periodicity but is highly erratic, it is under the influence of a so-called chaotic attractor.

In recent years chaotic behavior has been discovered in a wide variety of natural systems, and their mathematical modeling has made rapid progress. An entire discipline has sprung up within dynamic systems theory devoted to the study of the properties of chaotic attractors and of the systems governed by them; it became popularly known as chaos theory. Despite its name, the theory seeks to eliminate rather than discover or create chaos—it studies processes that appear chaotic on the surface but on detailed analysis prove to manifest subtle strands of order. Chaotic attractors are complex and subtly ordered structures that constrain the behavior of seemingly random and unpredictable systems. Several kinds of chaotic attractors have been discovered so far (including the Birkhof and the Shaw bagel, the Lorenz butterfly, the Rössler band, and the Rössler funnel, named after their discoverers and the geometric shapes they exhibit in the models); many more are expected to come to light in the near future. They reduce seeming chaos to complex varieties of order in processes as varied as fluids in flow and the blending of substances during solidification. The phenomenon of turbulence is a case in point: it has been known since the nineteenth century, but its origins have been imperfectly understood. By 1923 experiments in fluid dynamics had demonstrated the appearance of annular Taylor vortices; these appear when the speed of stirring in a fluid increases beyond a critical point. Further increases in stirring produce additional abrupt transformations and ultimately turbulence. Turbulence, however, can be modeled by chaos theory and proves not to be entirely chaotic: it exhibits the complex varieties of order inherent in systems governed by chaotic attractors.

The behavior of dynamic systems in the empirical world is normally influenced by many different attractors simultaneously; dynamic systems theory seeks to account for such systems by correspondingly complex models that, for the most part, are yet to be developed. But even the existing models simulate the behavior of real-world systems with surprising fidelity. The key feature of the behavior of the models is the analysis of the sudden phase change that leads empirical systems from one kind of stable state to another. In dynamic systems models, such changes in systems behavior represent bifurcations of the trajectory traced by the system states. Bifurcations appear in the "phase portrait" of the systems and consist of a shift from one type of attractor to another. In a shirt from a static to a periodic attractor, a hitherto stable system begins to oscillate, while in a shift from periodic to chaotic attractors, a previously oscillating system lapses into chaos. These so-called subtle bifurcations are but one variety of basic system changes; the other variety is known as catastrophic bifurcations and consists of the sudden appearance or disappearance ("out of the blue") of static, periodic or chaotic attractors.

Bifurcations in the complex systems mapped by dynamic systems theory have direct application to real-world systems. Subtle bifurcations can model increasing instability in third-state systems far from thermodynamic equilibrium. A system, such as a series of chemical reactions in stable equilibrium, begins to oscillate; or an oscillating system, such as a "chemical clock," becomes turbulent. In its mathematical models, dynamic systems theory identifies a number of such "scenarios" leading from stable equilibrium to chaos.

Models with catastrophic bifurcations (conducing from turbulent to newly ordered states through the reconfiguration of the attractors) simulate rapid evolutionary leaps with the greatest fidelity. The significant simulations occur when dynamic systems are destabilized and pass through a chaotic phase on the way toward essentially new—and in practice unpredictable—steady states. The chaotic phase is not entirely random even if it is highly erratic and unpredictable: it is governed by chaotic attractors. During this phase the bifurcating systems are sensitive to minute changes: the smallest variation in an initial condition can give rise to widely differing outcomes. (Dynamic systems theorists speak of "initial condition dependence" and illustrate this condition by interpreting the Lorenz butterfly—a pioneer chaotic attractor discovered by meteorologist Edward Lorenz in 1963—as a metaphorical "butterfly effect": if a monarch butterfly flaps its wings in Southern California, a month later Outer Mongolia's weather becomes unpredictably different. Since the world's weather is in a permanently chaotic state, the story is only slightly exaggerated.)

As the explorations of the great empirical realms of evolution in Part Two will show, subtle or catastrophic bifurcations, involving transitory chaotic phases in shifts from stable to chaotic and back to stable attractors, are the kind of transformations that underlie the evolution of all third-state systems in the real world, from atoms of the elements to societies of human beings.

SUMMARY

The main features of GES—the grand evolutionary synthesis—can be briefly summarized. Autocatalytic and cross-catalytic feedback loops predominate in open dynamic systems in the third state

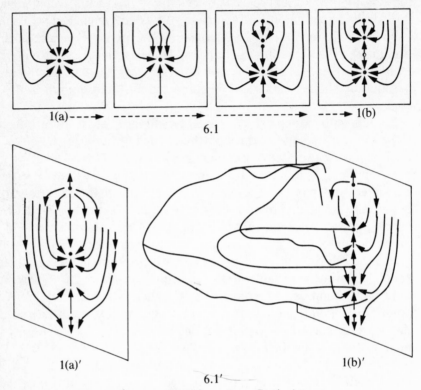

Fig. 6. *Catastrophic Bifurcations:* Static Attractors

In Figure 6.1′ the same catastrophic bifurcation is represented in a three-dimensional state space. (The state space is a geometrical model for the virtual states of the system. Each point in the state space represents a single, instantaneous state. As each state is characterized by a unique evolutionary tendency described by the velocity vector, a given initial state evolves along a unique trajectory. Following a transient response phase, this trajectory asymptotically approaches a limit set which is the system's attractor. The attractor may be static, periodic, or chaotic.) As Figure 6.1′ shows, the second static attractor appears "out of the blue," far from any other attractor (separatrices, the divisions between the basins of the attractors, are ignored for the sake of clarity).

Figure 6.2 shows a catastrophic bifurcation due to the sudden appearance of a periodic attractor. First one periodic attractor dominates the dynamics of the system in the center of its basin [2(a)]. Then, as the control parameters are changed, another periodic attractor appears out of the blue [2(b)]. Figure 6.2′ shows the same process in a three-dimensional state space, also without separatrices. (For details, see Ralph Abraham and Christopher Shaw, "Dynamics: A Visual Introduction," 1980, mimeo.)

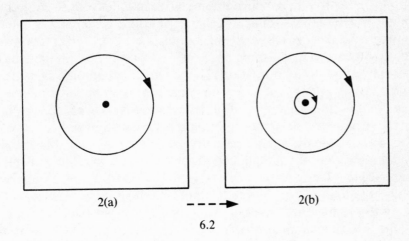

2(a)   - - - →   2(b)

6.2

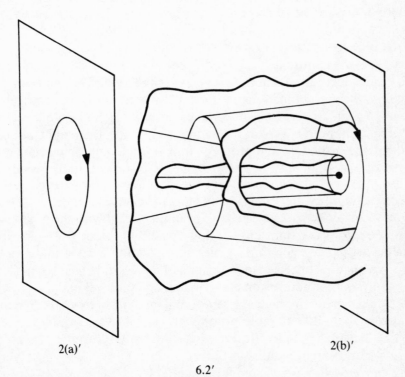

2(a)′   2(b)′

6.2′

Periodic Attractors

far from equilibrium in virtue of their rapid reaction rates and great stability. However, as no autopoietic reaction cycle is entirely immune to disruption, constant changes in the environment sooner or later produce conditions under which certain cycles can no longer operate. The systems encounter a point known in dynamic systems theory as a bifurcation. The outcome in complex systems, as both experiment and theory demonstrate, is essentially indeterminate: it is not a function of initial conditions, nor of changes in the environment. Bifurcations produce a basically random selection from among the set of alternative steady states available to the system through the amplification of some among the existing fluctuations. The new steady states assimilate the perturbations within the limits of error-tolerance of the catalytic cycles and are likely to produce increases in the complexity of system structure. There is a significant probability that the system leaps to a new plateau of nonequilibrium; that it retains a greater quantity of a more dense flux of free-energy for a longer time and thus becomes more dynamic and more autonomous in its milieu.

New levels of organization are attained in the system-forming process of evolutionary convergence as catalytic cycles on one level interlock and form hypercycles on the next. Thus molecules emerge from combinations of chemically active atoms; protocells emerge from sequences of complex molecules; eukaryotic cells emerge among the prokaryotes; metazoa make their appearance among the protozoa, and protozoa join in more embracing ecological, social and, at least in one instance, also sociocultural systems.

Continuity and consistency in the processes of evolution give rise to continuity and consistency in its products. Periodic destabilizations of systems far from equilibrium, coupled with the organizing effect of a constant energy flow, push bifurcating systems up the ladder of the evolutionary hierarchy, adding weaker and more flexible bonding energies to stronger and more rigid ones, complexifying system structures on each organizational level and simplifying them again on the next level, and adding highly developed control capabilities to more primitive forms of self-regulation.

The fact that systems in the third state evolve through periodically indeterminate nonlinear transformations toward regions ever further removed from equilibrium offers a first glimpse of the foundations of a grand evolutionary synthesis based on valid scientific theories. The main elements of GES are third-state systems within an energy flow maintained by catalytic cycles, the mix of determinacy and randomness introduced by the alternation of ordered dynamic stability with periods of indeterminate transformation, and the statistically significant tendency toward greater complexity and a higher level or organization, with more dense free-energy fluxes and decreased entropy in regions ever further removed from the inert state of thermal and chemical equilibrium.

In the late twentieth century the scientific understanding of the logic of evolution—the forms and dynamics of change in complex systems—is sufficiently advanced to permit a revival of the classical ideal of a grand evolutionary synthesis, now on a sound empirical footing. In our day the evolutionary paradigm is ready to move from metaphysics to physics—and to all the sciences of the empirical world. The exploration of the paradigm, and the creation, criticism, and elaboration of progressively more refined grand syntheses, is a challenge awaiting the contemporary community of natural, human and social scientists. It is a challenge well worth accepting, for the elaboration of a sound and detailed GES would surely rank among the greatest achievements of human intellectual history.

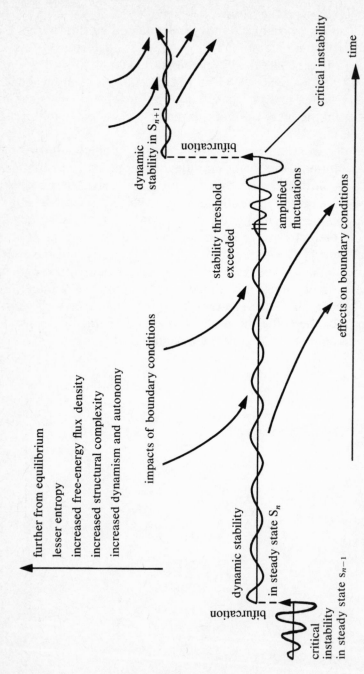

further from equilibrium
lesser entropy
increased free-energy flux density
increased structural complexity
increased dynamism and autonomy

impacts of boundary conditions

dynamic stability in S_{n+1}

bifurcation

stability threshold exceeded

amplified fluctuations

critical instability

dynamic stability

in steady state S_n

bifurcation

critical instability in steady state s_{n-1}

effects on boundary conditions

time

Fig. 7. *The Statistically One-Way Buildup of Dynamic Nonequilibrium Systems*

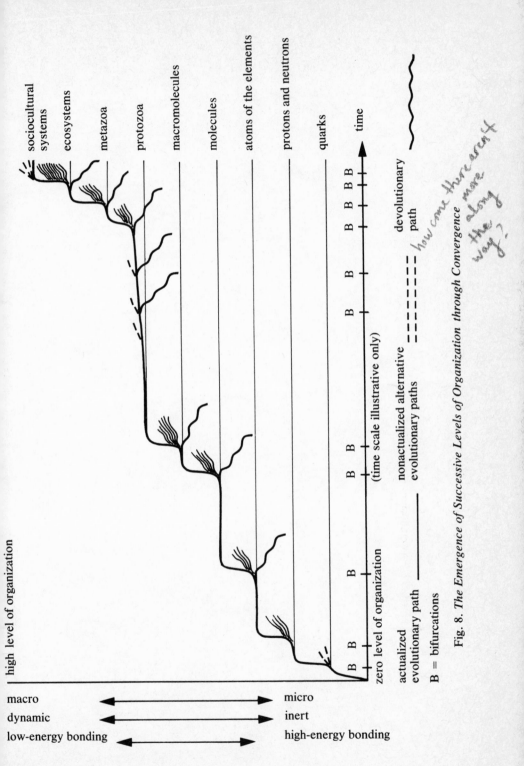

high level of organization

sociocultural systems
ecosystems
metazoa
protozoa
macromolecules
molecules
atoms of the elements
protons and neutrons
quarks

time

devolutionary path

nonactualized alternative evolutionary paths

how come there aren't more along the way?

(time scale illustrative only)

zero level of organization

actualized evolutionary path ——

B = bifurcations

B B   B   B   B   B B B

B B   B   B   B B

macro ←——→ micro

dynamic ←——→ inert

low-energy bonding ←——→ high-energy bonding

Fig. 8. *The Emergence of Successive Levels of Organization through Convergence*

Part Two

The Realms of Evolution

Introduction

Grand evolutionary syntheses remain products of the intellect, fascinating but abstract possibilities unless the processes and products they describe can be tested and verified in the empirical realms of observation. Not everything that is rational is also real [*pace* Hegel]; a grand synthesis may be coherent and intellectually pleasing yet unexemplified by, and thus inapplicable to, empirical reality. The proof of the pudding is in the eating: we must turn to the real world and its realms of evolution to test the validity of the synthesis outlined in Part One.

The realms of evolution in the empirical world do not follow classical disciplinary boundaries although they are logically aligned with the great divisions of empirical science: divisions between the physical, the biological and the social sciences. In the perspective of a grand synthesis these are not absolute and watertight divisions but sets of theories based on investigations of third-state systems located at different clusters of organizational levels. The physical sciences, more specifically cosmology and astrophysics, deal with the synthesis of matter-energy systems on the most basic levels of organization, beginning with quarks, hadrons, leptons, electrons and neutrons, and all elementary particles with rest mass. The biological sciences investigate more complex entities built of physical and physicochemical matter-energy systems, beginning with the nucleic acids that code the genetic information of living species. The social sciences in turn concern themselves with a still higher cluster of organizational levels, namely with the various social and cultural systems constituted by *Homo sapiens,* a particular kind of living species.

Each of these clusters of levels of organization is built on the cluster of levels below. Since the lower levels had to be already formed before the higher levels could appear, it is not surprising that the clusters emerged successively in time; the three great realms of evolution form not only an organizational, but also a temporal sequence. The synthesis of matter began about twenty billion years ago, an almost infinitesimal fraction of a second after the creation of the observed universe. Living systems emerged sometime between 4.6 and 3.6 billion years ago on the surface of our planet, although they may have originated earlier and may continue to emerge later on other planets. The age of the social and cultural systems created by sapients must be measured in tens of thousands of years; they date roughly from the emergence of our ancestors as a dominant species among the hominids.

The three clusters of organizational levels form a pyramid. At the base there are the physical and physicochemical matter-energy systems synthesized throughout the billions of galaxies that populate the universe. Above it are biological systems on earth, and presumably on a significant number of other planetary surfaces. At the apex of the pyramid are sociocultural systems formed on earth by sapients—and (probably) on other locations by extraterrestrial beings with the required forms of intelligence.

Logically, the investigation of the great realms of evolution must start at the base of the pyramid and at the beginning of the process: with the synthesis of matter in the physical universe.

The processes of cosmic evolution bring forth a variety of matter-energy systems; these systems define the range of constraints and the scope of possibilities within which systems on higher levels can evolve. Systems on the lower level clusters can permit the evolution, but can never determine the nature, of systems on higher-level clusters. As already noted, the laws of evolution are not deterministic but possibilistic; they do not select precise evolutionary trajectories but set the context within which nonequilibrium systems in the third state choose their own evolutionary destinies. The evolution of physical matter-energy systems sets the stage and specifies the rules of the game for the evolution of biological species, and biological evolution sets the stage and specifies the rules of the game for the evolution of sociocultural systems.

This first attempt to test the validity of the grand synthesis

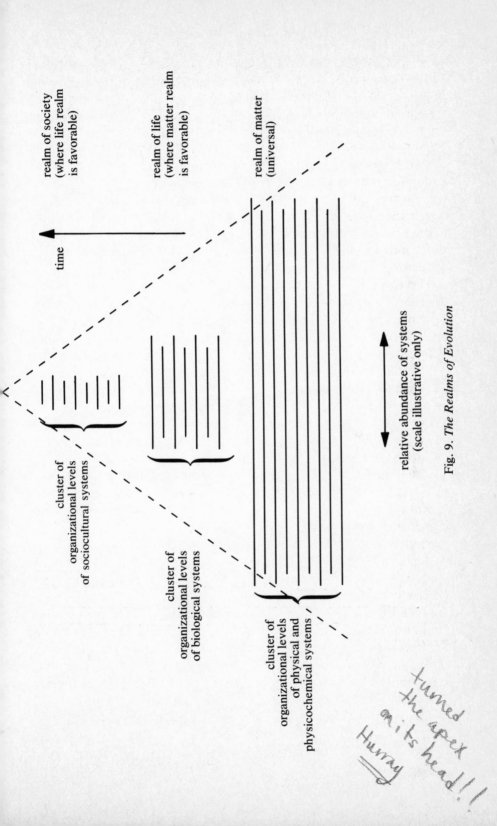

Fig. 9. *The Realms of Evolution*

realm of society
(where life realm
is favorable)

realm of life
(where matter realm
is favorable)

realm of matter
(universal)

time

relative abundance of systems
(scale illustrative only)

cluster of
organizational levels
of sociocultural systems

cluster of
organizational levels
of biological systems

cluster of
organizational levels
of physical and
physicochemical systems

turned
the apex
on its head!!!
Hurray

sketched in Part One will follow the pattern traced by evolution itself: it will start with a review of the evolution of matter in the cosmos, continue with the evolution of life in the biosphere, and conclude with the evolution—the patterns of development—of human societies in history.

3

The Evolution of Matter

We begin the exploration of the empirical validity of GES by going back to the scientific equivalent of Adam and Eve: to the beginnings of the evolution of matter in the universe. We go back to the logical starting point: the beginning of time and the beginning of space, the first and necessarily theoretical microseconds that marked the initiation of all evolutionary processes known to science.

THE ORIGINS OF THE UNIVERSE

The origins of the universe were the focus of philosophical and poetic speculation from the earliest myths to this day. Cosmology moved from the field of myth and metaphysics to that of science in the twentieth century, but it was only in the 1980s that major breakthroughs occurred in our understanding of the very earliest phases of the universe.

Grand Unified Theories (GUTs)

Contemporary cosmologists postulate new, unified and universal forces in a veritable mathematical *tour de force* to account for the observed features of the universe. According to current theories (the so-called GUTs and super-GUTs—grand and super-grand unified theories) the origins of the universe involve both a major discontinuity and the fragmentation of a fully integrated force field. Although GUTs and super-GUTs are still in rapid evolution and beset with as yet unresolved puzzles, theoretical cosmologists believe that the universal forces that govern cosmic processes are essentially unitary. Super-GUTs assume that during the first phases of the creation of the universe, a single unitary force governed all interactions. Then, as the universe expanded and cooled, this unitary force broke up into the familiar universal forces of gravity, electromagnetism, and the strong and weak nuclear forces.

Contemporary GUTs hope to achieve what Einstein tried to do four decades earlier: create a unified field theory. Einstein attempted to unify what he believed were the two fundamental forces in nature: gravity and electromagnetism. However, the strong and weak nuclear forces were discovered at about the same time, and by midcentury physicists were confronted not with two, but with four seemingly distinct forces.

GUTs became a respected scientific endeavor when the electromagnetic and the weak nuclear forces could be unified in the theory of the *electroweak force*. According to this theory, advanced by Sheldon Glashow, Steven Weinberg, and Abdus Salam in the late 1960s and confirmed only a decade later, at high temperatures these forces are one and the same. It is only at lower temperatures that the four bosons that carry the unitary electroweak force (the photon, the W^+, the W^-, and the Z^0) divide into the photon (carrying the electromagnetic force) and the other three (which carry the weak nuclear force). The particles were discovered in 1983, at the CERN accelerator in Geneva. Spurred by this success, physicists are intent on moving toward "grand unification" by integrating the strong nuclear force with the electroweak force in the *electronuclear force*. This version of GUT calls for a finite rest mass in the *e, mu,* and *tau* neutrinos—they could then transform into each other. But the theory will not be easy to verify: this level of unification occurs at extremely high energies. Proof may elude scientists in the laboratory, but could still be found in the particles left over from the Big Bang—the only event in the known universe that produced the required energies.

Theoretical physicists are now working on the final step known as supergrand unification: they seek to demonstrate the unity of the electronuclear force with the force of gravity. The mathematics of these "theories of everything" (TOEs) are often outlandish. In the theory of superstrings, for example, the computations call for a

Bah

universe of ten dimensions—physicists hope to reduce them eventually to four. Although TOEs are still speculative, most physicists agree that the derivation of a *grand unified force* requires the decay of the superheavy X-bosons within the first 10^{-35} second, owing to falling temperatures.

A *super-grand unified force* is assumed to have operated at temperatures of 10^{30} K, reigning until about 10^{-39} second in the current phase of the universe. When time advanced to 10^{-35} second the temperature dropped to 10^{28} K and a phase change took place in the expanding cosmos: below this temperature X-bosons could no longer be produced. As these bosons vanished the expanding cosmos developed a tension that, according to the GUTs, caused a rapid acceleration in expansion, that is, created the so-called inflationary phase. At the conclusion of inflation the X-bosons disappeared and the grand unified force fragmented into the electroweak and the strong nuclear forces. The cosmos resumed its more moderate rate of expansion.[1]

Inflationary Scenarios

The hypothesis of an inflationary phase can account for the observed isotropy and homogeneity of the universe. The distribution of photons, for example, is isotropic (that is, the same in any direction) within a limit of accuracy of one part in ten thousand. Yet only those regions that are less than two degrees apart could have been in contact with each other when photons decoupled from radiation. Thus the 2.7 K background radiation, filling space evenly, seems a puzzle. To account for this "horizon problem" and related problems in Big Bang cosmology, Alan Guth proposed the inflationary scenario. The first formulation of the theory, in 1981, proved to be fatally flawed; but the "new inflationary scenarios" advanced since 1983 by the Russian physicist A. D. Linde, among others, appear to better conform to observational evidence.

The flatness, homogeneity, isotropy, and baryon asymmetry of the universe, the existence of galaxies, and the absence of monopoles and domain walls are now explained in the new scenarios. They offer an especially ingenious solution to the problem of isotropic background radiation. Before inflation the region of the

primordial universe that inflated into the known universe is conceived to have been small enough to produce thermal equilibrium.
Employing complex and admittedly speculative theoretical devices
(such as a special type of Higgs potential to allow a smooth phase
transition through a large-scale supercooling effect), the new inflationary scenarios postulate a chaotic phase of random fluctuation
following the initial instability, followed by the rapid inflation of
one of the fluctuation "bubbles" into the known universe. Density
fluctuations inside the bubble are thought to have been negligibly
small; the inside space was almost homogeneous. The exponential
expansion extended this homogeneity to all of the observable
universe. At the same time long-wave quantum fluctuations of
curvature and of the scalar field are believed to have grown
rapidly, introducing the density perturbation necessary for the
subsequent formation of galaxies. (An entirely "wrinkle-free"
early universe could not have produced the inhomogeneities that
subsequently led to the gravitational contraction of matter into
galaxies.)

According to the inflationary scenarios the universe underwent a
phase change prior to settling into the kind of order we observe
today. The phase change consisted of the following sequence of
states:

1. *An initial state* of net zero energy (a "vacuum") during
   which neither time nor space were measurable in relation to
   time and space in the subsequent epochs
2. *A transitory chaotic state* of an indefinite (and immeasure-
   able) duration, consisting of random fluctuations and "bubbles" (induced possibly by a critical instability of the initial
   state)
3. *A short-lived inflationary state,* lasting 10^{-33} second, during
   which one of the bubbles nucleated and inflated by a factor
   of 10^{20} to 10^{50}
4. *A consequent dynamically ordered state* lasting to date
   some 10^{18} seconds (about 20 billion years) in which the
   known universe thins and cools and creates third-state
   matter-energy systems progressively further from thermodynamic equilibrium.[2]

THE SYNTHESIS OF MATTER-ENERGY SYSTEMS

To explain the generation of matter in cosmic space-time is a basic aim of contemporary cosmology. Cosmologists now assume that the energy of the vacuum from which the known universe originated has split and transformed into positive energy, which is matter, and negative energy, which is the energy of the gravitational field. As the energy of the field is transferred into matter energy, material systems come into being. An irreversibility is introduced into the structures of the universe that did not exist in the standard model produced by Einstein in 1917. However, the solutions of Einstein's equations were shown to suggest an unstable universe by Friedman in 1922; Hubble's observations confirmed the recession of the galaxies; and the discovery of residual black-body radiation testified to the thermal evolution of the cosmos. Irreversible processes began to assert themselves in the forefront of cosmological speculations.

In a new hypothesis Prigogine and Géhéniau attempt to reconcile the concept of an irreversibly evolving universe with Einstein's field equations. They postulate a new equivalence, complementing relativity theory's equivalence of matter and energy: this is the equivalence between matter and entropy. If matter is created from the vacuum, the entropy of the latter must have been zero: when matter is created, entropy is also produced. The entropy necessary to generate matter proves to be gravitational entropy.[3] If the new hypothesis is valid, the universe is self-creative in its very nature. Evolution in the form of the irreversible creation of matter becomes one of its fundamental characteristics.

The matter-content of the contemporary cosmos is but a fraction of the matter created in the first fractions of a second following the Big Bang. The observed universe consists entirely of that segment of matter that survived the very early phases in virtue of a slight imbalance between matter and antimatter. The decay of the X-bosons appears to have yielded a surplus of one proton for every billion pair of protons and antiprotons. This residue (one-billionth part of the originally created matter of the universe) survived the pair-annihilation process and became available for further evolution in cosmic space and time.

Temperature and Density Parameters

The ongoing evolution of matter in the cosmos represents the transfer of energy from the gravitational field, governed by the action of universal forces and the changing parameters of the expanding universe. Two factors of change are of special importance: the temperature and the density of the cosmos.

When the inflationary phase ended, the density and the temperature of the cosmic fireball were too high to permit the formation of systems of any kind. Both these values moved in a range that is humanly unimaginable. A universe younger than 10^{-24} second had densities greater than 10^{50} grams per cubic centimeter [g/cm^3] and temperatures in excess of 10^{20} degrees on the Kelvin scale.

However, this intense and dense sea of radiation soon provided a milieu for the emergence of the first microparticles. At already $<10^{-11}$ second quarks must have existed, although details of their creation are still lacking. At about 10^{-11} second and 10^{15} K temperature, hadrons (protons, neutrons, and mesons) are believed to have formed. They were created by "pair-creation"—the opposite of the process of pair-annihilation. (In pair-creation, particles emerge from clashes among packets of energy, in a way opposite to that in which colliding particles and antiparticles—protons and antiprotons—annihilate each other and yield pure energy.) As density and temperature decreased further, fewer and fewer hadrons were created; the dominant process became the breakdown of the existing hadrons into high-energy photons.

After about a millisecond the superenergetic conditions required for hadron-creation and annihilation had almost subsided, and lighter particles, called leptons (electrons, neutrinos, and muons) began to predominate. A whole class of elementary particles was created under conditions where the average temperature had decreased to "merely" 10^{10} K and the average density was around 10^{10} g/cm^3. By the completion of the first millisecond, most of the leptons, too, had broken down into photons: the cosmos was still too hot and dense to permit the formation of enduring matter-energy systems. The matter content of the cosmos had thinned once more: whatever particles survived this epoch did so as a microscopic precipitate within the macroscopic sea of radiation that still filled space and time.

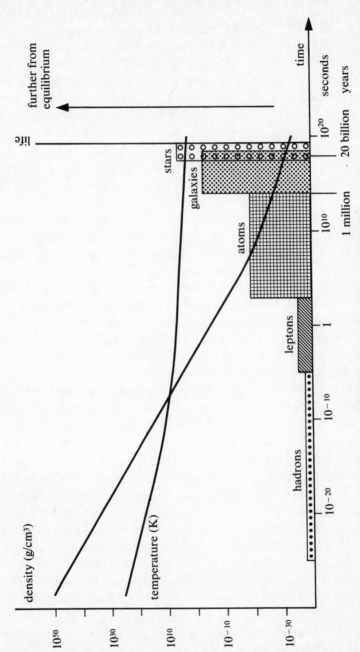

Fig. 10. *Density and Temperature Parameters in the Buildup of*
Matter-Energy Systems

The universe continued to cool and thin, and allowed the surviving particles to become electromagnetically linked. Hydrogen was the first element to be created, consisting of the linkage of but one negatively charged electron with one positively charged proton. When temperatures have dropped to about 10^9 K, protons and neutrons interacted to produce deuterium, an isotope of hydrogen. As deuterium interacted in turn to produce helium, some 20 to 25 percent of the hydrogen component of the universe was converted into helium. The helium-creating process may have lasted only a few minutes. By the time a sufficient number of helium nuclei had been created to produce heavier elements through interaction, the temperature of the universe had fallen below the threshold value of 10^8 K.

In the epoch between the first few thousand years and one million years, most of the charged particles clustered electromagnetically into atoms. At the one-million-year mark, these systems began to contract and form vast galaxies.[4]

The epoch of galaxy formation may have lasted about five billion years. Midway through this epoch the density of the cosmos decreased by another factor of more than a billion, to 10^{-20} g/cm^3, and average temperatures dropped to about 300 K. As soon as the galaxies were essentially complete, perhaps already one billion years after inflation, stars began to form.

Stars are created by the gravitational clustering of matter within the galaxies. But stars not only form within the vast galactic reaches; once formed; they also evolve. First-generation stars begin their life cycle with the already synthesized matter of the universe: they consist of about 90 percent hydrogen and 9 percent helium nuclei, with traces of other elements. Initially they have but a small temperature gradient between core and surface. But as stars evolve, the temperature of the core increases and therewith the temperature gradient between core and surface. Nuclear fusion in the core synthesizes the hydrogen nuclei into helium, and then into heavier elements. Relatively massive stars—equal to or more massive than our sun—evolve significantly and, at the end of their life cycles, explode (more exactly, implode and rebound) as supernovae. Stars below the critical mass evolve less radically, toward a luminous, relatively stable and cool state.

The remarkable fact of stellar evolution is that it sets forth, in a constant and irreversible manner, the formation of matter-energy systems in the universe. Not only do stars produce progressively heavier elements in their hot interiors, even their final explosion synthesizes additional heavy elements in interstellar space. First-generation (population II) stars mainly convert hydrogen into helium. Second- and third-generation (population I) stars carry the process further: these stars start their active life cycle not only with hydrogen but also with elements such as iron and magnesium, and they build up further heavy elements. The synthesized elements ultimately find their way into interstellar space. Even the cooler and less massive stars inject the elements synthesized in their interiors into surrounding space; they continually lose their outer layers in low-velocity stellar winds and occasionally eject deeper layers in bursts of activity that produce planetary nebulae.

The statistically irreversible buildup of matter in the cosmos results in a rich soup of elements that undergoes further evolution in successive generations of stars and enriches vast interstellar clouds. The more dense among these clouds are known to contain heavy substances including various organic molecules such as formaldehyde and hydrogen cyanide.[5]

In today's relatively cool (2.7 K) and thin (approximately 10^{-30} g/cm^3) universe, the synthesis of matter-energy systems continues. Progressively heavier elements are produced, including oxygen, nitrogen, and carbon—elements essential for the evolution of life. As hydrogen is present as well, it is probable that in many places the universe harbors matter-energy systems we would call living. Wherever suitable energy and density conditions are given—that is, on the surface of planets similar to earth associated with a star similar to our sun—the evolution of complex molecular systems is likely to begin. The thermal and chemical conditions for this process are known: there must be a variety of atoms capable of forming chemical bonds (mainly carbon, hydrogen, nitrogen, oxygen, and also phosphate and sulphur supplemented with some metals and halogenes); the temperature must not exceed 100°C; and there must be a continuous energy irradiation. With about 200 billion stars in our galaxy and some 10 billion galaxies in the universe, chances are good that a significant number of stars have planets that meet these specifications. Since the abundance and distribution of chemical elements are much the same in all parts of the universe, the probability that there are a considerable number of planets with matter-energy systems that qualify for the predicate "living" is by no means negligible.[6]

The universe is at the same time more complex and more unitary than we had reason to believe until very recently. It consists of a gravitational field of enormously high initial energy which cools, expands, and brings forth a great variety of nonequilibrium matter-energy systems. (Neutrons, protons, electrons, in fact all particles with a positive rest mass are already in a state of nonequilibrium; only photons with zero rest mass are an exception.) As field energy is transferred, and due to expansion density and temperature decrease, an increasing variety of material particles are created. This is followed by the synthesis of more complex structures still further from thermodynamic equilibrium, such as atomic nuclei. Gravity condenses these matter-energy systems into galaxies, which subsequently produce radiant stars. Within the hot interior of stars, heavier elements are constantly synthesized, and the supernovae that mark the end of massive stars produce the temperatures required for the synthesis of still heavier elements. The building of matter-energy systems continues with the gravitational contraction of already enriched interstellar matter and the formation of second- and third-generation stars. Stellar and interstellar matter becomes sufficiently enriched to initiate the synthesis of nonequilibrium systems in the third state on planetary surfaces with a suitable chemical composition and a constant energy flux within the permissible range.

THE ARROW OF TIME IN THE COSMOS

The Radiation-to-Matter Energy Transfer

On the assumption that the energy of the vacuum from which the cosmos originated has split into a positive segment which is matter and a negative segment which is the gravitational field, the creation of matter involves the transfer of the energy of the field to the energy of matter. Given that the universe expands and cools, the radiation which was predominant in the field diminishes while matter is continuously built up. In the expanding and cooling universe *energy is irreversibly transferred from radiation to matter*. The arrow of time in the cosmos is given by this irreversibility. As energy is more and more concentrated in matter-energy systems, these systems move into the third state, further and further from thermodynamic equilibrium.

The transfer of energy from radiation to matter can be calculated with mathematical precision. The energy transferred is expressed as energy density, that is, as unit of energy per unit of volume. First the energy density of the background radiation is calculated, and then it is shown how this relatively low quantity (equivalent to 2.7 K) changes over time. The formula allows the extrapolation of a curve that traces the decrease of the energy density contained in pure radiation from the first fraction of a second to any subsequent time in the history of the universe.

Next the energy density retained in matter is computed, and its change over time is plotted. Since energy is constant while the universe is expanding, the density of energy in the cosmos (whether unbound in radiation or retained in matter-energy systems) decreases over time. But, because radiation, unlike matter, is affected linearly by the Doppler shift (that is, by the recession of the galaxies), the energy density unbound in pure radiation decreases faster than the energy density bound in matter.[7]

The difference in the decrease of energy density in pure radiation ($\rho_r c^2$) and in matter ($\rho_m c^2$) makes for a net and continuous transfer from radiation to matter. The process can be plotted in the form of two curves; these intersect sometime between 50,000 and one million years after the initial inflationary phase of the universe. (The variance is due to uncertainties in determining the precise amount of the energy density of matter.)

Viewed in these terms, the course of cosmic evolution becomes logical and clear. During the first microseconds, the gravitational field of the universe consisted almost entirely of radiation. As the universe cooled and thinned, matter-energy systems came to be synthesized and energy became increasingly bound in matter. When the energy-density of radiation and of matter matched, matter decoupled from radiation: photons and free electrons could no longer interact. The universe as a whole moved into thermal disequilibrium. It created flows of energy between energy-radiating macrosystems, such as active stars, and various types of microsys-

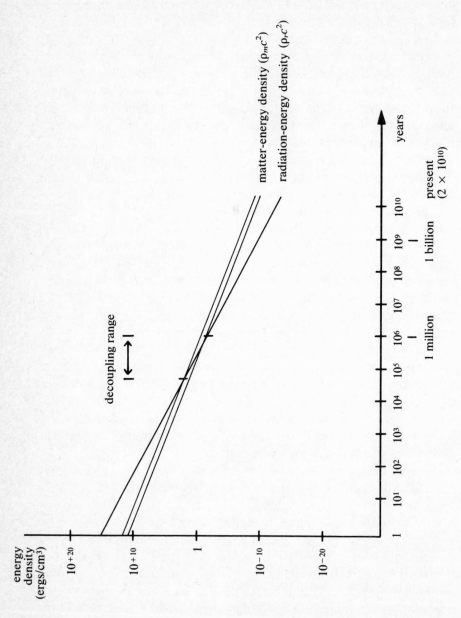

Fig. 11. *The Decrease of Energy Density in Radiation and in Matter*

tems engulfed in the flows in regions such as interstellar clouds and planets. Some among the many energy flows proved to be the engine of evolution for matter-energy microsystems of ever increasing dynamism and complexity.

The differential between the energy density of matter and of radiation increases over time. The structural complexity and dynamism—in other words, the negative entropy—of the microsystems grow proportionately to this differential. When these systems reach a critical phase of negentropy, they no longer behave as systems in the first state *in* equilibrium, or as systems in the second stage *near* equilibrium, but as systems in the third state *far* from the equilibrium state. Immersed in an energy flux, they do not go linearly to equilibrium but maintain structure and complexity in dynamic steady states. They may also increase their level of nonequilibrium by moving into alternative, still more structured steady states following critical perturbations.

As third-state systems move further into nonequilibrium the density of the energy flux captured and retained by them increases. While the average energy density of matter in the cosmos decreases (although slower than the energy density of radiation), the net energy transfer from radiation to matter creates energy flows that trigger the evolution of dynamic systems that go counter to the cosmic average in retaining an increasing amount of free energy per unit of mass.

The evolution of matter in the universe is thus assured. Out of a disequilibrated cosmic space-time field come matter-energy systems in the third state, progressively more negentropic, more complex and dynamic, and further removed from thermal and chemical equilibrium.

The synthesis of dynamic matter-energy systems exploring ever further reaches of nonequilibrium continues today, some 20 billion years after the original instability that marked the beginning of cosmic space and time. While no new galaxies are being formed, within those that exist new generations of stars are born and massive older stars implode and fly apart in supernovae or collapse into black holes. Stellar and interstellar matter is irreversibly enriched with heavier elements. The stage is thus constantly prepared for the emergence of the still more structured matter-energy systems that we associate with the phenomenon of life.[8]

The progressive structuring of systems is likely to occur throughout the reaches of the cosmos; the process is triggered by the energy flows created in virtue of the progressive transfer of energy from field to matter. While this creates the basic preconditions for the evolution of matter, it does not determine just *how* matter evolves—its precise evolutionary trajectory. Even if the thermal and chemical evolution of stars is likely to be basically similar in all galaxies, significant differences could occur in the trajectories traced by more complex nonequilibrium microsystems. Elsewhere in the cosmos macromolecules, cellular, supracellular, ecological and possibly even sociocultural systems may emerge in forms considerably different from those which they assume on earth.

4

The Evolution of Life

The evolution of life on earth began with initial conditions provided by evolution in the cosmos. That cosmic evolution created precisely those particles, atoms, and molecules that it did determined the range of possibilities and the parallel constraints for the evolution of biological species, but it did not determine their exact forms. Living systems define their own evolutionary trajectories. They are neither determined by nor reducible to physical and chemical systems and processes.

Biological evolution is not merely cosmic evolution on a planet; it would be naive to search for products and processes that are identical in the two realms. Yet the general laws that govern the evolution of all systems in the third state remain invariant as we pass from the cluster of organizational levels prevalent in the universe at large to the cluster occupied by living systems in the earth's biosphere. We can test and explore this invariance by reviewing recent discoveries concerning the origin of life, the nature of macroevolution and of mutation, and even the emergence of *Homo sapiens*.

THE ORIGINS OF BIOLOGICAL EVOLUTION

According to current estimates, biological evolution on this planet began over 3.6 billion years ago. Fossils with traces of advanced chemical evolution dating back 3.4 billion years have been successfully identified; primitive biological organisms have been shown to have existed at least 2.8 billion years ago, and evidence of the biochemical activity of prokaryotic cells with

71

modern enzyme structures has been uncovered in fossils 2.3 billion years old.

Statistical studies show that the probability of the accidental appearance of self-reproducing systems of linear polymers is extremely small; at the same time experimental evidence indicates that whenever certain chemical and energetic conditions obtain systems similar to primitive forms of life are synthesized. Most scientists now accept the view that under the particular conditions that reigned on earth some 4.6 to 3.6 billion years ago, life arose necessarily rather than as a result of some cosmic accident.

Theories of a purely accidental (not to mention extraterrestrial) origin of life, popular in recent years, are unduly speculative. The chemical constituents required for the evolution of life were present on earth before biological evolution took off. The six elements that make up some 98 percent of matter in the cosmos— hydrogen, helium, carbon, nitrogen, oxygen, and neon—and even the more complex molecules essential for the synthesis of the first self-replicating cells, were already synthesized in the physical universe. Even amino acids and nucleic acids were (and are) synthesized; they are known to be present in meteorites. We now know that the universe itself produces the basic building blocks of life, and that some of these building blocks could have found their way to the surface of the youthful earth, carried most likely by grains of dust from dense interstellar clouds.

Conditions on earth were ideal for the abiogenic synthesis of the chemical constituents of life. Monomers like sugars, amino acids, purine, and pyrimidine bases, and linear polymers built of these monomers, such as proteins, nucleic acids and other macromolecules, must have been synthesized in the constant energy flow from the sun and from the hot magma of the earth's core. The chemical composition of the planetary surface was a thermodynamically mature template capable of initiating biological processes. It absorbed solar and geothermal energy, stored and used some—initially minuscule—part of it in matter-energy structures, and radiated the rest into space.

The constant flow of energy from the sun to earth, and from the interior of the earth to its surface, must have had the effect of organizing the elements of the "chemical soup" on the surface into protobionts: systems capable of capturing and storing ever more of the free-energy flux. Experiments show that in a system containing the main bioelements (carbon, oxygen, hydrogen, nitrogen, phosphorus, and sulfur), the energy of visible and ultraviolet light triggers a series of photochemical reactions the end result of which are various compounds of medium molecular weight.

Experiments that seek to reproduce the origins of life in the laboratory have chalked up an impressive record since the pioneering efforts of A. I. Oparin in the 1930s. By the 1950s Stanley Miller and Howard Urey conducted path-breaking studies in which they exposed a mixture of water vapor, methane, ammonia, and hydrogen gases to electric discharges. They found that after a week organic compounds emerged, including D and L amino acids. The nucleotides which make up DNA and RNA molecules eluded detection until the early 1980s, but then C. Ponnamperuma used improved detection techniques and found that, together with the amino acids, all the bases that form DNA and RNA molecules are synthesized as well. Experimenters note that the forces of intermolecular attraction and the tendency of certain molecules to form liquid crystals leads to the spontaneous synthesis of large and complex molecules. Such reactions are known to take place in free solution in water as well as when the molecules adhere to particles of clay. Indeed, the presence of clay orients the reactions in a direction consistent with the evolution of life.

The latest hypothesis concerning the origins of life is not the result of laboratory experiments but of theory combined with observation. It is the work of John Corliss and his co-workers who, after detailed submarine researches, suggest that life originated in shallow Archean seas owing to the eruption of magma through cracks in the earth's crust. Biological evolution on this planet took off, it appears, with the selection of the most rapidly growing and replicating primitive cells within submarine hot springs that acted as small steady-state flow reactors.

Indeed, submarine hot springs are packed-bed, mixing-gradient, continuous-flow chemical reactors. They consist of a cracking front, where sea water is heated rapidly to appr. 600°C, carbon is extracted from the rock, and reactions with ferrous iron produce a reduced fluid containing methane and hydrogen. The fluid reacts and equilibrates with the rock as it mixes with sea water and cools to about 350°C. The equilibrated fluid then either rises directly to the sea floor or mixes in the rock with cold sea water to emerge at lower temperatures (5°–30°C), following a specific, highly constrained mixing process. High-energy monomers could be synthesized in the fluid at or near the cracking front, and then rapidly quenched by mixing. The mixing trajectory would "freeze" the thermal energy into high-energy molecular bonds. Fractures in the upper parts of the hot springs would provide a suitable environment for the synthesis of clay minerals. The presence of clay would extract and accumulate organic matter, achieving high concentrations from an initially dilute aqueous solution. The steady flow within the hot springs would provide a constant supply of energy-rich molecules, including high-energy organic molecules and a variety of oxidized and reduced inorganic molecules and ions.

There is considerable evidence that flow reactors of this kind may be the ideal site for the emergence of dynamic systems in the third state. Katchalsky and Prigogine show that flow reactors constitute classic reaction-diffusion systems basic to the thermodynamic description of self-organizing behavior, while Eigen suggests that they can generate autocatalytic cycles of interacting protein and nucleic acid fragments. Corliss contends that submarine hot springs (which still exist, though in smaller numbers than in the early history of the earth) were the reactors that led to the evolution of the most rapidly growing varieties of cells, that is, those with the most efficient autocatalytic cycles.

In time some of the emerging cells became linked by hypercycles into interacting cohorts. As one species of cell produced material necessary for the growth of another, and the other in turn produced material for the growth of the first—or of a third, which in turn became a link in a chain that fed back to the first—all changes that would destroy one unit in the chain would have destroyed the entire chain. The full chain, however, was richer in information than any of its components and could adapt to conditions that would have proven fatal to the units separately. Thus the evolutionary cycle that took off with catalytic cycles linking protocells and molecules continued with hypercycles linking cells in multicellular systems.

Once evolved, life became almost entirely independent of geothermal energies. Although some marine organisms (giant tube worms, mussels, clams, and crabs) still live in symbiosis with bacteria on geothermal energies at great ocean depths—up to 2,500 meters—life on earth is now sustained by the flow of energy from the sun. Plants use sunlight in photosynthesis, converting water and carbon dioxide into carbohydrates; animals eat plants and other animals. The flow of energy remains, however, an essential engine of all processes in the biosphere. Were the energy differential between the surface of the sun (currently approximately 6000° C) and the surface of the earth (about 25°C) ever to equalize, not only life, but all thermodynamic processes on this planet would soon come to an end. The heat stored in the earth's atmosphere would be depleted in a few months, while that in the oceans would be dissipated already in a matter of weeks. Worms, clams, and bacteria at the bottom of the deepest seas would be the sole survivors.

THE DYNAMICS OF BIOLOGICAL EVOLUTION

Speciation

Until the 1980s most life scientists held that the emergence of new species—now known as "speciation"—was essentially correctly grasped in the Darwinian framework, at least in its modern variant known as the synthetic theory. However, an increasing number of biologists are now questioning this conception. Their theories differ from the synthetic theory in several important ways. First, they contest the element of chance that governs the Darwinian account.[1] Biologists now find it difficult to see how a basically random search among a vast number of possibilities could have resulted in the emergence of the empirically known complexity of the living world. Michael Denton, for example, asks whether it is credible that random processes could have constructed an evolutionary sequence of which even such basic elements as a protein or a gene are complex beyond human creative capacities. How can one account statistically for the chance emergence of systems of truly great complexity, such as the mammalian brain—when even 1 percent of the connections in such a brain, if specifically organized, constitute a larger number of connections than the world's entire communications network! Chance mutations acted on by natural selection could well account for variations *within* given species, but hardly for successive variations *among* them.

The classical synthetic theory is in difficulty also when it comes to describing the tempo and mode of evolution. Some paleobiologists attack the classical conception that natural selection, acting on individuals, is gradual and continuous. They claim that "phylogenetic incrementalism," associated with the name of Darwin, is incorrect. They point out that Darwin himself professed incrementalism more from a conservative predisposition than on the basis of scientific evidence. In Chapter 15 of *The Origin of Species,* Darwin declared, "Natural selection . . . can produce no great or sudden modifications; it can act only by short and slow steps." Darwin followed Linnaeus in affirming, *"Natura non facit saltum."* Sudden leaps in nature resemble discomfortingly sudden changes—even revolutions—in human society, and the dominant mentality of Darwin's time extolled piecemeal adjustments and abhorred wholesale transformations. As current biographical researches show, Darwin was most likely influenced by the dominant mentality of his time. Nature, however, disregards the dispositions of nineteenth-century Englishmen and progresses by sudden leaps and deep-seated transformations rather than through piecemeal adjustments. In 1972, almost one hundred and twenty years after the original publication of *The Origin of Species,* Jay Gould and Niles Eldredge came out with a seminal study ("Punctuated Equilibria: an Alternative to Phylogenetic Gradualism") that introduced the leap into neo-Darwinian biology.

In the theory of punctuated equilibria—where the concept of equilibrium means a dynamic balance between species and environment and not thermal or chemical equilibrium—evolutionary processes concern entire species rather than individual reproducers and survivors. Evolution occurs when the dominant population within a "clade" (a set of species sharing a similar adaptive plan) is destabilized in its milieu and other species or subspecies that emerged haphazardly on the periphery break through the cycles of dominance. At that point the stasis of the epoch is broken, and there is an evolutionary leap from the formerly dominant species, threatened with extinction, to the peripheral species or subspecies. The process is relatively sudden: "speciation"—the emergence of new species—punctuates long periods during which existing spe-

I'm not so sure...

cies persist basically unchanged and no new species establish themselves.

As long as a species persists, it remains relatively unchanged: its genetic information pool is handed down basically preserved to succeeding generations. Gaps in the fossil record do not indicate a gap in the record of continuous, piecemeal evolutionary changes but signal periods of perhaps many millions of years during which species did not evolve significantly. New species tend to burst on the scene within much shorter time frames: somewhere between 5,000 and 50,000 years. The alternation of long periods of stasis with sudden evolutionary leaps prompted the biologist D. V. Ager to liken the history of life on earth to the life of a soldier: it consists of long periods of boredom interspersed with short periods of terror.

The theory of punctuated equilibria is considerably different from traditional Darwinian theory despite the occasional affirmation that it is basically Darwinian evolution applied to entire species rather than to individuals within species. Although the theory does not specifically question the accidental nature of mutations (which may make it inadequate to explain the emergence of vast complexity and higher organizational levels within the known time frame of evolution on earth), the distinction between a continuous and a discontinuous mode of evolution is by no means negligible. The classical synthetic theory knows no sudden instabilities and sudden phase changes; the theory of punctuated equilibria, however, affirms them. The new theory recognizes the occurrence of long periods of stasis, during which the catalytic cycles that maintain organic species in their environments perform adequately and correct for a limited range of perturbations, and it claims that when the epochs of stasis come to an end, evolution is sudden and unpredictable in detail.

According to this "saltatory" theory, the rate of speciation is strongly influenced by the survival patterns of competing species. Species capable of surviving under a relatively wide range of environmental conditions (including a variety of climates, topologies, predator and prey populations, etc.), speciate less often than those which are fitted into narrower niche structures, or "environmental ruts." When many highly specialized species coexist within a clade in ruts that differ only slightly from one another, relatively small changes in the niche structure can knock out particular populations. "Specialists" speciate under many conditions where "generalists" can still adapt and survive. The diagram of the branching tree of life no longer resembles the continuous Y-shaped joints of the synthetic theory; it is now pictured in terms of abrupt switches, from dominant species which become extinct to hitherto peripheral ones that become dominant, with short life lines for specialists and comparatively long ones for generalists.[2]

Not only do species appear in sudden transformations within a clade, but entire genera make their appearance in bursts of creativity that mark given paleological epochs. For example, some 600 million years ago the Cambrian explosion brought into being most of the invertebrate species within the relatively brief span of a few million years. According to recent conceptions the explosion was triggered when the previously dominant community of algae (consisting of prokaryotic cells) was destabilized by the appearance of single-celled eukaryotes that fed on the algal community. By cropping the algae they broke through the epoch of stasis that had persisted for billions of years. The algae were destabilized; niches for additional species were created; and subspecies that emerged on the periphery could move in to occupy them. A large variety of prokaryotes appeared, and these in turn made possible the emergence of more specialized eukaryotes which functioned as their "predators."

Mutation

In order for new species to emerge not only need new niches be available, also mutant populations must be at hand to exploit the available niches. Mutation, an essential element in the Darwinian synthetic theory, remains a cornerstone of the new biology. While proponents of the theory of punctuated equilibria no longer view the emergence of new species as a direct consequence of natural selection acting on mutant individuals, mutations transmitted by reproducing individuals remain a key factor in creating the alternative species or subspecies that achieve dominance when the previously dominant species in a clade become critically destabilized.

Contemporary microbiology finds that mutation is a considerably more complex process than previously envisaged. The process

time

generalist   specialist
species

Fig. 12 *Speciation in Biological Evolution*

is open to influence from the environment and it, too, is saltatory, occurring through a phase change in the genome.

The genome—the specific genotype of an individual—contains the genetic program with the necessary information to interact with environmental factors within and external to the organism and to determine the (permanent or transient) characteristics of the phenotype. Biological organisms are maintained in the environment through the reliability of the information coded in the genome. The phenotype (the actual organism) is the outcome of the interaction between the information-based instructions carried by the genotype and the relevant factors of the external environment. A mutation, then, is an alteration of the individual's genome that in turn produces an altered phenotype and thus alters the genotype of the species.[3]

While each species has the capacity to transmit the content of its genotype from generation to generation, assuring the reproductive invariance of its species, mutations can change the sequence of nucleotides in the genome of any given individual. The nucleotide strand, arranged as a double helix, is endowed with considerable degrees of conformational flexibility. The folding of the nucleotides has to be extremely accurate; for example, in the average human diploid nucleus the length of the nucleotide sequence is about 1.7 meters—fitted inside a nucleus with a radius of 2.6 micrometers. (The length of the strand in the double helix is thus 650,000 times the radius.) Recent findings indicate that the required accuracy is not rigid: different configurations are possible and physical factors, such as humidity, temperature, and ionic strength, among others, exercise an influence.

In higher organisms only about 20 percent of the nucleotide sequence of the double helix is sufficient for assuring the coding and regulatory function of the genome. The remaining 80 percent appears to be useless for such purposes; in fact it is often called the "silent DNA." The silent segment consists of a high degree of repetition of certain sequences with a scattered distribution throughout the genome. This may be crucial in mutations since it may allow sudden genetic variation through a translocation of elements in the nucleotide sequence and through quantitative changes by means of an increase or decrease of nucleotides. The genome, it appears, mutates through sudden phase changes induced by changes in the silent DNA.

The nature of transformations in the genome is the subject of intense investigation. Some scientists envisage shocks faced by the genome to which it responds in a programmed manner. Sensing mechanisms, it is believed, alert the genome of imminent threat, and the genome responds by restructuring itself, assuring its own survival as well as that of the cell. Such restructurings produce mutant individuals which in turn can lead to speciation when populations of mutants enter into competition with other species within a clade.

The genome itself proves to be a nonlinear chemical system far from equilibrium. It maintains its structure in a continuous flow of matter and energy through numerous self-regulatory and replicative processes, including autocatalytic cycles. And it undergoes sudden phase changes when challenged by "shocks" or other destabilizing changes in the values of some critical parameters.

The new findings of microbiologists concerning the nature of mutations, and the new theories of paleobiologists concerning the tempo and mode of evolution, add up to fresh insights into the dynamics of biological evolution. There is still an element of chance, but there is also pattern and regularity. The response of the genome to environmental perturbations cannot be predicted in detail; even in the most sophisticated theories of microbiology the outcome of mutations remains random. Likewise the outcome of the macroevolutionary processes of speciation remain unpredictable. However, the laws that govern biological evolution conserve their validity throughout the range of individually unpredictable processes. Biological evolution unfolds in a lawlike manner in that, independently of specific detail, when changes in the niche structure critically destabilize a dominant species in a clade, the destabilized species yields dominance to the mutant species or subspecies produced by phase changes in the genome.

Convergence

In order to understand how evolution climbs ever higher on the cluster of organizational levels in the realm of life we have to add another factor to speciation and mutation: the factor of convergence. Convergence—the tendency of third-state systems to form hypercycles in a shared milieu—introduces the element missing in mainstream biological theory and removes the puzzle of how high levels of complexity can be achieved in relatively short time frames. Hierarchization through hypercycles—in other words, the principle of convergence—accounts for biological evolution's climb to higher organizational levels: it shows that the outcome of the processes of mutation and speciation is not entirely random but follows a pattern observed in all realms of evolution.

The effects of convergence can be traced throughout biological evolution. Already in the early history of life eukaryotic (nucleated) cells evolved through convergence among prokaryotic (non-nucleated) cells. (Many of the vital organs of eukaryotes, such as mitochondria, chloroplasts, flagella and the mitotic apparatus, may have originated as hypercycles formed among primitive prokaryotes.) Multicellular species, in turn, emerged out of hypercycles among the eukaryotes. On still higher levels, entire ecosystems resulted from hypercycles among multicellular species. Life continually explores novel combinations of structures and functions as existing species interlock their catalytic cycles in shared habitats and jointly converge in higher-level systems.

The benefit of evolutionary convergence toward high organizational levels is the dynamism and autonomy available to hierarchically organized systems. Roughly at the level of protocells, autopoietic systems appear—the hypercycles evolve the ability to replicate the entire cell structure. Cell division renders single-celled organisms theoretically immortal: they can replicate themselves as long as boundary conditions remain favorable. Additional autopoietic functions appear when species converge on the multicellular level of organization. The reproduction of the entire organism is invented to compensate complex nonequilibrium phenotypes for their individual mortality. Reproduction in the bisexual mode becomes a source of variety within species; through the mechanism of recombination it assures that there are individuals fitted to a large variety of niches.

In the trend toward dynamism and autonomy the key innovation, for which the multicellular level of organization is sine qua non, is endothermy: a constant and high internal body temperature. The typical temperature of 37° C stores considerable free energy and allows a wide range of activity with speed, variety, and stamina. A constant input of free energy-containing substances and a dependable elimination of waste products maintains the homeostatically stabilized "milieu interieur" of complex warm-blooded organisms. The entire metabolic process is precisely regulated on the highest, controlling level by catalytic cycles and norm-maintaining negative feedbacks, enabling the organism to compensate for variations in its external environment.

While the benefit of evolutionary convergence is increased dynamism and autonomy, the cost is increasing vulnerability. For example, the body temperature of mammals is close to the upper threshold of permissible temperatures for most living protoplasm. Also, the survival range becomes dramatically reduced: while a cold-blooded organism can tolerate a wide range of temperature conditions (some fish can recover even after being frozen), warm-blooded animals must be able to maintain their body temperature within a few degrees from the norm, or succumb.

Convergent evolution to higher and higher organizational levels involves a gamble: the exchange of relatively simple and reliable catalytic cycles for complex, hierarchically organized sequences of dynamic individual- and species-maintaining hypercycles. The kind of stability typical of the simplest forms of life (such as blue-green algae and other prokaryotes) is surrendered, and its absence is compensated for by highly sophisticated feedbacks coding multi-level self-regulating mechanisms. The gamble means greater dynamism and autonomy—but at the cost of the mortality of the individual and the risk of sudden destabilization and ultimate extinction for the species. The fossil record testifies to the poor odds in this gamble: more than 96 percent of the biological species that at one time populated this planet have ultimately disappeared.

The arrow of time in biological evolution points toward increasingly dynamic and autonomous species. At the same time it points toward species that are highly complex and vulnerable, forced to rely on delicate survival functions that include, in higher species, not merely genetically coded and inherited behavior, but also learning acquired in the lifetime of the individual. The gamble can pay off—for a time at least. *Homo* is living proof of it.

THE EMERGENCE OF *SAPIENS*

Although there is no single universally accepted theory of the origins of our species, it is probable that the ancestral tree of the family of man exhibits the same punctuated, saltatory mode of evolution as other forms of life. The divergence of hominids from the apes sometime between four and eight million years ago is itself a relatively sudden event: within a matter of a few million years an erect, bipedal species emerged, leaving behind the tree-dwelling apes.

The mutation may have been due to increased dryness during the Pliocene when East African tropical forests receded and were replaced by more open savannahs. An upright posture would have been advantageous in tall grasses, and bipedalism would have freed the arms for the use of tools and for wielding weapons in confrontation with large, savannah-dwelling predators. The earliest hominids may have spent some of the time in the trees and some on the ground, moving toward full bipedalism in stages. In any case the ancestors of *Homo* were full-time bipeds already two million years ago.

Our direct ancestors are likely to have evolved through a rapid and saltatory speciation—a true bifurcation—within the hominid group. There is no firm evidence of gradual evolution within any hominid taxon. *Sapiens* does not appear to be the result of a gradual series of adaptive mutations within a single lineage such as *africanus—robustus—boisei—sapiens*. It seems likely that neither *robustus* nor *africanus* evolved into *boisei,* nor indeed did *boisei* evolve into either *africanus* or *robustus*. Paleoanthropologists are faced with a number of puzzles in the interpretation of recently discovered fossils, but seem generally disposed to regard *afarensis* as the common ancestor of *sapiens* and other, now extinct hominid species. Should this be the case, some three million years ago *afarensis* would have speciated into four distinct hominid lineages *(habilis—erectus—sapiens, robustus, africanus,* and *boisei)* and have done so within the remarkably brief span of 300,000 to 500,000 years. For now scientists can only speculate on the reasons for this rapid radiation: it could have been caused by a change in the climate, by changes in competing species or some other variation in essential parameters. In any case, *afarensis,* the then-dominant hominid species, seems to have been rapidly destabilized in its environment and replaced by various mutants that emerged on the periphery. If the hypothesis is correct, then the lineage that gave rise to *Homo* exhibits the same kind of saltatory bifurcation that is characteristic of the evolution of all systems in the third state, whether they are in the physical, the biological, or even the social realm.

Once a species has burst on the scene, it appears to have remained basically unchanged throughout its existence. *Erectus,* our direct ancestor, lived in various geographic locations with but minor variations for a million and a half years. In its much shorter span, *sapiens,* too, has been essentially unchanged. The seeming continuity of evolution hides a series of discontinuities, as species disappear and others take their place. In the case of the hominids, it was *sapiens* that survived, while the others became extinct.

We now have reasons to believe that modern man became a dominant species only recently. While our ancestors were present in Africa already 100,000 to 130,000 years ago, it was only some 30,000 years ago that they achieved dominance in Europe. It was around then that Neanderthal man disappeared, and his disappearance, while still shrouded in mystery, may have had much to do with the appearance of sapiens. There is no record of any hominid species but *Homo sapiens* in Europe during the last 30,000 years. The fossil record indicates that sapiens migrated from Africa about five thousand years beforehand and may have initially coexisted with the Neanderthals, possibly on different locations. But as sapiens spread into East Asia and as far as Australia, the major competing species vanished, creating another puzzle for anthropologists. Did the sudden shift in Europe come about because sapiens could better adapt than Neanderthals to the warming trend that made for the appearance of forests in place of the great steppe? The answer is not clear. Yet the fact seems indisputable: sapiens invaded from Africa and became the sole hominid species in Europe within the brief span of five thousand years. This is yet another instance of saltatory evolution through the destabilization of a dominant population and the subsequent rise to dominance of a species invading from the periphery.

Changing conditions in the biosphere favored the preservation of the traits of *Homo sapiens* and his spread as a dominant species to the inhabitable parts of the continents. A species capable of conscious thinking, symbolic communication, and complex social organization emerged as the supreme predator of life on earth.

But the appearance of modern man was not without risks: our species entered into the evolutionary gamble in a grand way. It entrusted its individual and species survival more and more to the perception and interpretation of the environment, and less and less to intrinsically stable physiological mechanisms and genetically coded behavioral patterns. So far, the gamble paid off: *Homo* is still alive and dominant. But he now lives within sociocultural systems that he no longer knows how to control. His future will be decided by the evolution of these still higher-level systems—more exactly, by his ability to steer the course of their evolution.

Although biological evolution on earth culminated in some sense in *Homo,* there is nothing predetermined about the appearance of our species—no final cause or general plan that would lead to man by design or by necessity. Biological evolution, like the evolution of all third-state systems in the empirical world, does not determine the course of its unfolding but merely identifies the possibilities and sets the constraints. Notwithstanding the many specific features of the evolution of life, it shares its basic mechanism with all other forms of evolution. Speciation, the sundering of one coherent, integrated and reproductive community into two (or more) species, is a bifurcation in the evolutionary path of a lineage. Similarly to bifurcations in all dynamic systems, the outcome of individual speciation processes are indeterminate and unpredictable; all we can tell is that the emerging species will be better fitted into its milieu (that is, will have greater reproductive success) than its predecessor. But despite the individual unpredictability of the particulars of emerging species, there is an overall, statistical predictability associated with the historical course of macroevolution itself: the set of all speciations in the last four billion years manifests a definite convergence toward higher organizational levels. This process does not necessarily lead from protocells and algae specifically to *Homo,* but it does lead from systems that are relatively simple, microscopic, and comparatively close to equilibrium toward systems that are further from equilibrium, larger in size, greater in complexity, and more dynamic and autonomous.

Evolution is not teleological; it does not have a precise goal in the form of any particular species of organism or ecosystem. Yet it is directional in that it drives systems in the third state progressively further from equilibrium into the high-level and nonlinear realm where life appears, and possibly intelligence.

5

The Evolution of Society

The hypothesis that the laws governing the evolution of natural systems also govern the development of human societies is intrinsically reasonable. These laws do not prescribe the course of evolutionary development but merely set the rules of the game— the limits and the possibilities that the players themselves exploit. The rules for biological evolution have been set by evolution in the cosmos. For sociocultural evolution the rules could have been set by biological evolution, first and foremost by the evolution of *Homo sapiens*.

The hypothesis does not mean that human societies are biologically determined. It means only that societies are evolving systems emerging and persisting within the multiple-level structure of other systems in the biosphere. Societies follow the rules set by the general laws that govern the evolution of such systems within the limits and possibilities created by human beings, their values, beliefs, habits, and mores. But societies follow these rules on their own, typically societal level, and not on the biological level of their members.

The hypothesis, though not biologically reductionist, does draw on concepts and theories developed in part in the natural sciences. It thus raises the specter of perennial controversies between natural and social scientists concerning the application of the postulates of natural sciences to the sphere of human affairs. Historians, especially, have traditionally considered their field a record of historical events and not the exemplification of universal processes. History, they say, deals with the unique, the individual, and the concrete; it also deals with events infused with human will and purpose. By contrast, the natural sciences deal with the universal, the general, and the abstract, and their subject matter is untouched by conscious purposes. The natural sciences postulate laws to predict and if possible control phenomena; but prediction is impossible in the realm of history and control is often undesirable.

As already noted in Chapter 1, in the history of Western civilization the split between the natural sciences and the humanities goes back at least two hundred years. But this split is now transcended by fresh knowledge coming from the sciences of complexity, laying the foundations for a unified, grand conception of the evolution of third-state systems in physical nature, in living nature, and in history. However, contemporary historians and social scientists are seldom fully up to date on these developments. The scientific laws known to the great majority of historians are deterministic and mechanistic; they are basically the laws of Newtonian physics. Historians are justified in objecting to their application to the events and processes of history. It is to be regretted, however, that merely a handful of historians realize that the laws of evolution are not mechanistic and deterministic, and thus that—in principle at least—they are by no means inapplicable to human and social structures and processes.

In any case, the applicability of evolutionary concepts and laws to the development of human society should not be prejudged. Whether or not human society changes and develops according to the laws that govern the evolution of natural systems cannot be answered by abstract logical analysis. In order to decide the validity of the hypothesis we must confront some of the basic concepts of the sciences of complexity with historical facts and empirical observations. While this project obviously cannot be completed on these pages, I can outline the basic evolutionary axioms of a theory of society and explore whether or not they apply to characteristic and significant features of historical development.

THE EVOLUTIONARY AXIOMS

1. Society is a system composed of groups of human beings in specific relations. The social system—much like an organic population, a clade, or an ecosystem—maintains itself or changes independently of the particular destinies of its individual members. Human beings pass through it in cycles of birth, maturation, and

death; society persists, develops, or decays according to processes that take place on its own societal level. The fact that the individual members of human societies are conscious, language- and tool-using persons specifies but does not determine its evolutionary dynamics; it only introduces the specific control parameters that set the range of possibilities and the nature of the constraints in the behavior of the social system.

2. A dynamic system in the third state, society occupies a cluster of organizational levels above those of third-state systems in the physical and biological realms. The social system's environment is both natural and social: it is in part the biosphere and its various ecologies, with the sun as the main energy source and surrounding space as the main energy sink, and in part the sociosphere, made up of other societies and their infrastructures.

3. Society is neither a natural system, like an atom, a molecule, or a cell, nor an artificial system such as a machine or a computer. It is the result of human action and interaction, but not of conscious human design. Unlike specific organizations (corporations, public and private institutions, armies, churches, professional associations, social clubs, and so on), the networks of relations that bind individuals in entire nations, states, and cultures cannot be designed; they emerge in the course of history. The degree of complexity attained in a modern society, though modest in comparison with an organism, exceeds by far that which its human members could achieve by purposeful design.

4. Society, though composed of human beings, is not reducible to the sum of their behaviors and attributes; it evolves functions and acquires attributes that are typical of its own, societal levels of organization. Such spontaneously emerging features include the capacity to replicate principal components (human individuals as well as groups and associations of individuals) and to renew any part of the structure that may have been impaired by internal or external fluctuations. Self-organization is another feature of society. Like other third-state systems, society is a self-evolving system in its own right, capable of settling into alternative steady states following critical perturbations. Through autopoiesis and bifurcations, society maintains itself in its particular milieu and, if viable, evolves alternative structures and organizational forms in the course of time.

5. Notwithstanding the suprabiological organizational levels of

society, its structural complexity—though far greater than that of organizations and other artifacts—is less than that of its individual members. (The human brain alone is more complex by several magnitudes than all the societies of the contemporary world put together.) The relative simplicity of sociocultural systems is consistent with general evolutionary trends. Systems on a higher level of organization are initially always simpler than the systems that constitute their main components; a new organizational level creates a simplification and not a complexification of system function. (The comparative simplicity of sociocultural systems is readily explained by comparing the biological time scale with the time span of social history. The origins of the genus *Homo* go back millions of years; the origins of human societies as sociocultural systems, rather than as tribal reproductive units, go back merely twenty or thirty thousand.)

6. Society evolves through convergence to progressively higher organizational levels. As the flows of people, information, energy, and goods intensify, they transcend the formal boundaries of the social system. The catalytic cycles that maintain the system in its environment encounter similar cycles in the intersocietal milieu and interact with them. In time the cycles achieve coordination as intersocietal hypercycles. Thus neighboring tribes and villages converge into ethnic communities or integrated states, these in turn become the colonies, departments, provinces, states, cantons, or regions of larger empires and ultimately of nation-states. When empires are stripped of their far-flung territories and overseas colonies, the capital regions and the liberated states are open to new forms of convergence among themselves. (In today's world this process leads to the creation of various regional and functional economic and political communities and blocs among developed as well as developing nation-states.)

These evolutionary axioms apply to society because society forms a third-state system on the suprabiological cluster of organizational levels. Society is such a system because human beings have evolved as social creatures: they tend to behave with some measure of coherence. Coherence results not because of some metaphysical property that makes humans into collaborative social animals, but because prolonged interaction among individuals leads to the emergence of an overall order that is not the conscious aim of any of them; and this order is conserved and handed down to successive generations through the patterns of value, belief, and custom prevalent in society.

The historically evolved social orders are constantly shaped by individual action and interaction and modified by changes in collective culture and public policy. The orders impose constraints on individual behavior, although these constraints are perceived as such only if they are out of phase with the values, expectations, and general cognitive map of individuals. In a relatively stable, unstressed state of society, the constraints imposed by the spontaneously evolved social order appear as accepted forms of social intercourse. They bond individuals within kinship, community, or interest groups. In traditional societies myths and religion create the main kinds of social bonds, while modern societies produce many types of bonds and allegiances, cemented not only by mores and customs but also by legal and juridical systems and various rules governing public and personal behavior.[1]

THE DIRECTION OF SOCIAL EVOLUTION

Society, a dynamic but relatively simple suprabiological system, evolves in a fuzzy and generally disordered manner—so much so that students of history often question whether there is any pattern underlying the sequence of historical facts and events. History, as positivists claim, seems to be "one darn thing after another." Yet if we place the here outlined axioms in the context of a sufficiently large cross-section of historical development not only can we perceive basic patterns in history, but we can perceive that these patterns are consistent with the general direction and the dominant dynamics of the evolution of life in the biosphere—and likewise with the evolution of matter in the cosmos.

The people of ancient civilizations have perceived patterns in the way societies exist and evolve millennia before social scientists ever posed the question. Agrarian societies, strongly dependent on the weather and thoroughly integrated in their natural environment, believed in a cyclical pattern, following the seemingly eternal recurrence of the seasons. Classical societies sometimes perceived themselves as having descended from an earlier golden age: the pattern they perceived was no longer circular but traced a descending slope. When notions of progress became more firmly established, societies qualified the eternal recurrence of the circular pattern with the image of an ascending helix: all things recur, but they do so on a higher level. It was only in modern times that the dominant pattern in historical development was conceived as an arrow with an irreversible, upward direction of flight.

The pattern indicated by the evolutionary hypothesis is progressive but not linear. It resembles a fluctuating graph with many local peaks and valleys but with an ascending tendency. The state from which, and that toward which, it ascends can be best elucidated by comparing the earliest known stage of historical development with the latest stage. The progression from Paleolithic to modern times is highly uneven, with countless forward leaps and sudden regressions, yet it exhibits an overall direction. The structure of Stone Age tribes is considerably less complex than the structure of modern nation-states. More important, as we shall see, Stone Age tribes are systems with a far more limited capacity to access, store, and use dense fluxes of free energy in their environment than modern societies.

It is clearly an oversimplification to base arguments for directionality in history on a comparison between Stone Age tribes and modern nation-states. But these two types of social systems represent the temporal poles of societal development known in history. Recorded history begins with Stone Age tribes and extends, to date, to modern nation-states. In the intervening epochs, despite temporary regressions and deadends, structural complexities have grown and the dynamism and autonomy of societies have increased.

Technology as Engine of Change

The question of the motive force behind the observed general progression in history can be answered relatively unambiguously. Although the progression is not smooth and continuous, and it is not predetermined in any of its phases, it does exist, and its engine is technology. Technology has to be broadly conceived—as is customary today—as the instrumentality that imbues all human activities and extends human powers to act on nature and interact with others.² A technological innovation is not just the invention of a tool, but the stretching of the imagination and the transformation of common sense. A major technological breakthrough makes the supernatural natural—as, for example, with the mastery of fire and then of flight—and renders the abnormal and the unthinkable normal and even commonplace—as with a nuclear reactor or the instantaneous transmission of image and sound. It challenges people's values and practices and shakes the foundations of established institutions.

The impact of technology on society is generally proportionate to the flexibility of the dominant modes of social organization, that is, to the ability of society to apply internally or externally generated innovations. Stone Age societies were enduring but extremely rigid; they had little capacity for adopting (and perhaps even for coming up with) innovation of any sort. They maintained themselves by a fixed system of rites, rituals, and taboos, and corresponding myths and belief systems. The Paleolithic or Old Stone Age takes up much of the history of the hominid species, beginning first in Africa during the Lower Pleistocene some 1.75 to 2 million years ago. It took perhaps 1 million years for its primitive toolmaking to spread to Europe and Asia. The earliest technologies were simple physical implements: natural stones with little or no modification, or stones unifacially or bifacially flaked for chopping, bashing, or pounding, with some flakes for skinning and scraping. The social structures were limited to small family groups hunting and gathering together in open savannah country.

By the Middle Pleistocene human artifacts became somewhat more sophisticated and specialized: there were cleavers, points, hand axes, choppers, scrapers of various sizes, points, and related implements. In the early Upper Pleistocene hunting became selective, and more functional implements appeared: wooden spears and throwing and digging sticks, and in some regions the use of animal bones and antlers as tools. But it was only during the last 35,000 to 40,000 years in the Upper Paleolithic that greater advances were made, including knife blades, projectile points of stone and bone, antler for spears and darts, needles, chisels, spearthrowers, and harpoons, among others. The bow and arrow came into use toward the end of the Paleolithic as hunting became specialized and geared to the seasons and one or two species of prey.

Through nearly two million years, the precursor species of *Homo sapiens* lived a stable existence in close symbiosis with the environment. Except for causing the extinction of a few intensely and efficiently hunted species toward the end of this period, the ancestors of man did not ruin or unbalance either their environment or their own social structures and practices. The size of the communities remained small, and the division of labor may have been indistinct, as hunting and gathering are likely to have been cooperative activities that left little time for more specialized pursuits. But the slow yet persistent improvement of Stone Age technologies permitted populations to spread over vast, in part previously uninhabited areas.

The size of communities and their ways of life changed markedly with the advent of the Neolithic, around 8,000 years ago in the Levant. The cultivation of grain and the domestication of sheep and goats heralded a major technology-triggered revolution in society. It did away with the need to follow the source of food in small bands and transformed social rituals, values, and beliefs. Nomadic tribes were settled in permanent abodes and could grow more populous; a growing segment of the population was freed from the arduous tasks of hunting and gathering food and could take up social and even cultural pursuits. By the seventh millennium B.C. these advances had spread into eastern Europe, and by the third millennium up the Danube and across to the Atlantic coast. (While the new technologies appear to have spread into the Nile Valley and India as early as the fifth milennium B.C., they had no impact on the lifeways of large segments of the populations of eastern Asia and sub-Saharan Africa until about the first millennium B.C., owing to the bountiful environment provided by savanahs and forests.)

A technological breakthrough with equally vast consequences proved to be the invention of writing. It made possible the transmission of knowledge and experience, and the creation of far-flung empires with complex systems of taxation and sophisticated administrative structures. It also accelerated the spread of the other technologies, and the institutions, values, and beliefs that accompanied them.

In the span of the last millennium the tempo of social change has greatly accelerated. The effects of technological innovations have been amplified by rapid means of transportation and communication and exported by dominant economic powers and conquering armies. The archaic empires could maintain themselves for centuries—some for millennia—in favorable natural environments, mainly in river valleys such as the Nile, the Ganges, the Tigris-Euphrates, and the Huang Ho. But empires invented not only the means to produce food and administer far-flung territories; they also invented the technologies of conquest and subjugation, supplementing the power of human muscle with lances, arrows, and swords. Empires spread their dominance over ever-vaster distances and greater populations.

As William McNeill points out in his classic *The Rise of the West* (1963), the early structures of civilization displayed essentially the same characteristics wherever they evolved. They were agriculturally based hierarchies organized around cities and united into empires. They made use of written languages, had religions that were employed even more for political than for spiritual purposes, and maintained armies as well as modest scientific and technological establishments. The four or five empires that dominated civilization in the ancient world retained these basic structures for millennia.

In the Middle Ages, however, the classical structures broke down at the western edge of the civilizational pattern. In Europe, new technological developments, the relative weakness of the form in which the pattern was embodied, the peculiar attributes of the barbarian invaders, and certain features of the Greco-Roman tradition conspired to destabilize societies. During the period that encompassed the Renaissance, the Reformation, and the emancipation of science, European societies underwent a major transformation.

The causes of instability in Europe were multiple, some with long historical roots. For a long time after the ending of the barbarian invasions, Europe had enjoyed a modest but unrelenting growth in population. By the middle of the thirteenth century the bonds created under feudal society became strained. When the Black Death struck in 1348, a period of economic expansion was suddenly arrested and many of the bonds were permanently ruptured. The destabilization of European society is recorded in the attack of nominalist philosophers on the hitherto uncontested medieval world picture, and in the progressive independence from papal power of the political institutions nourished by the church for its own purposes. As technological innovations such as the compass, sturdy sailing ships and gunpowder were introduced, voyages of discovery extended the spiritual horizons of medieval Europe. They soon gave way to voyages of conquest, which in turn led to economic and political expansion.

Europe in transformation became the force that propelled the rest of the world out of its classical stability and into a new and uncertain future. Europe itself was in turmoil; the way to the modern age was not found without chaos and experiment. Religious reformers attempted to reestablish a pristine form of Christianity, while Renaissance scholars strove to revitalize civic humanism in the classical mold. But there were also scientific minds such as Galileo, Bruno, Copernicus, Kepler, and then Newton, who spearheaded a movement that led to the emancipation of science from medieval dogma. Modern science, with its insistence on observation and experiment, created a "purified" image of the world that, while perhaps simplistic in its mechanistic assumptions, proved to be eminently suitable for practical applications. As European societies realized the potential of autonomous science to "wrench the secrets of nature from her womb" and transform nature for human ends, a new technology-impelled revolution got under way.

The "first industrial revolution" created new relations between man and man and between man and nature, destabilized established institutions, and reformed traditional value and belief systems. It displaced traditional occupations and opened up new ones. The villages lost ambitious young people and impoverished peasants to new urban and industrial centers, where the former could occasionally rise on the ladder of status and wealth while the latter were forced into the sweatshops and "dark satanic mills" of the new industrialists. Gradually, through slow and often painful adjustments, better institutions emerged, mainly on the capitalist but later also on the socialist pattern. They restabilized medieval princedoms, kingdoms, and tsardoms as modern industrial societies.

This is way off — completely missing — the important things

Hardly consolidated, the industrial revolution was rocked by two world wars. These cataclysmic events, in addition to loosening established orders and institutions, promoted the discovery and application of several new technologies that soon moved from the military to the civilian sphere. The new technologies of information, automation, and communication heralded another transformation: the "second industrial revolution." Its impact on society was as profound as that of the Neolithic revolution, and infinitely faster. Complexity, based on the availability and rapid communication of information, grew in every domain. A tertiary sector of services emerged beside the traditional sectors of agriculture and industry. The mass media achieved an unprecedented level of influence. Wherever they penetrated the technologies of information, automation, and communication revolutionized every aspect of life in society.

In the span encompassed by Paleolithic societies on the one end and modern information-based societies on the other, an entire succession of societal forms has unfolded. The nomadic tribes of the Paleolithic transformed into the settled villages of the Neolithic; these in turn gave way to archaic empires and to local kingdoms and city-states. The classical empires were followed by medieval princedoms, and these yielded to the rise of nation-states, some with vast colonies. Today the colonies have disappeared, and modern nation-states have spread to the four corners of the world.

This historical succession of societal forms and types is capable of myriad interpretations, depending on the features and factors one chooses as one's point of departure. In light of the axioms we adopted to define the principal characteristics of society, the basic factor is not the variation in the adopted political, legal, and economic systems. These systems may vary in any historical epoch between the opposite poles of distributed power and democracy on the one hand and concentrated power and dictatorship on the other, between individual ownership and unconstrained markets on the one extreme and heavily structured and constrained forums of exchange on the opposite. Rather, the basic and noteworthy factors in the historical progression are the ways a society performs its autopoietic and evolutionary functions. These factors concern the interplay between technology—broadly defined—and the established social institutions and practices. The historical succession is best conceptualized in terms of the transformation of dominant technological types, and the structural and institutional changes catalyzed by them.

With attention to both the technological and the social factors we can perceive a series of dynamic transformations in the development of societies. Nomadic hunting-gathering tribes domesticate plants and animals and transform into settled agrarian-pastoral societies; agrarian-pastoral societies evolve such technologies as irrigation and crop rotation and transform into agricultural ones; agricultural societies develop handicrafts and simple manufacturing technologies and thus transform into industrial societies; and industrial societies, under the impact of new, mainly information- and communication-oriented technologies, evolve into postindustrial societies.

The evolutionary vision perceives history's arrow of time flying along the axis: hunting-gathering → agrarian-pastoral → agricultural → preindustrial → industrial → postindustrial society. The flight of the arrow may be interrupted at any point; it may be temporarily halted at any point; and it may be made to skip a stage at any point. But it may not, except under the impact of unusually powerful external factors—enduring foreign domination, long-term climatic changes with adverse effects, and the like—be fully and steadily reversed.

There is a sense to the terms *progress* and *development* in history. They denote an ineluctable advance of society along an evolutionary axis, sparked by technology. Technological change pushes societies along the here-noted trajectory, for technological change is irreversible on the whole. Societies progress mainly by creating, assimilating, or adapting technological revolutions, and technological revolutions, whatever their precise nature, always move from the hoe to the plow and not the other way. Only those technological inventions are adopted and handed down which represent an improvement in the efficiency of some procedure: greater speeed, less investment of time and money, and operation on a larger scale. This was true throughout the range of technological innovation from the wheel of agrarian society to the steam engine of industrial society, and it remains true today in the passage from the diesel engine of industrial society to the silicon chip of the postindustrial one.

However, the adoption of a new technology did not and does not necessarily mean an immediate advance in energy intensivity and efficiency. Classical Greece and Rome, for example, knew many more technologies than they actually employed; the institution of slavery discouraged the introduction of energy- and labor-saving devices. Although there were mines, clocks, and gadgets of various kinds, neither animal power nor the power of water and wind was effectively harnessed. Not even the vacuum and water pumps devised by Hero were used to alleviate human labor. On occasion specific pecuniary or political considerations blocked the adoption of a new technology. Emperor Tiberius destroyed the formula for glass that was said to be unbreakable and had its inventor put to death; he feared that unbreakable glass would undermine the value of gold, silver, and precious stones. Emperor Vespasian paid the inventor of an efficient system of pulleys and levels designed to lift and carry stone pillars but then had the model wrecked and prevented its use; he was concerned that the labor displaced by the device would create social unrest.

Economic, social, and political considerations can prove to be stronger than considerations of efficiency in use; also, the dominant values of a civilization can discourage the practical application of technological inventions. Gunpowder was invented by the Chinese but was used only in fireworks to mark ceremonial occasions; and the compass, another Chinese invention, had to wait for the coming of Western navigators to find practical employment. Neither the classical Mediterranean nor the ancient Chinese civilization valued energy efficiency, and both thought the design and use of mechanical devices unfit for soldiers, scholars, and other persons of standing and distinction.

In modern times as well, technological choices are often dictated by considerations other than improvement in energy efficiency. The range of technologies that waste energy and raw material is well known. But it is less widely known that even the gasoline engine, that bulwark of modern life, was chosen over the steam engine for reasons that had nothing to do with its competitive energy efficiency: when the Stanley Steamer and the four-cycle

Otto engine competed for acceptance, the Stanley Steamer was unexpectedly handicapped by an ordinance that called for the removal of the water troughs that were to resupply it along public roads. The reason had little to do with comparative efficiency: it was an outbreak of foot-and-mouth disease among U.S. cattle.

Although some technological inventions are never adopted, and those that are adopted are not necessarily the most efficient, all inventions that *are* adopted represent some measure of improvement in an activity or procedure. The refusal of societies to adopt technologies that actually reduce energy efficiency makes for directionality in history. It is the barb that keeps the wheel of societal change from spinning backward; the bowstring that propels the arrow of time forward.

In the late twentieth century we are in an era of growing societal dynamism achieved mainly through gains in energy efficiency. The information and communication technologies of the second industrial revolution do more with less: they allow significant energy savings by making use of far more dense energy fluxes than the technologies of the first industrial revolution. They combine with the exploitation of new and abundant energy sources, such as nuclear and to a lesser extent solar energy. A nuclear and renewable energy using technological society governed by a computer-elaborated flow of information is both more energy intensive and energy efficient than a society based on the burning of fossil fuels. It is further along the road of evolution than any of its historical predecessors.[3]

The trend toward the exploitation of increasingly dense and abundant energies is likely to continue, despite crises, bottlenecks, and short-sighted policies. Nuclear fusion and solar-voltaic technologies are already in intense development, and they assure access to superabundant sources of energy. Fusion liberates the energy contained in lithium and even common sea water; solar technologies convert the energy of the sun into electricity by the use of an abundant material such as silicon. The conception of the planet as a finite container of free energies is demonstrably false. All matter-energy systems bind energy in some way; it is only a question of human ingenuity to find the way to unlock the systems and make use of the liberated energy.

Because technological innovation in society is on the whole

irreversible, the arrow of time in history is consistent with the arrow of time in the physical and in the biological realms of evolution. Technological societies set forth the evolutionary progression toward more dynamic and autonomous systems by exploiting increasingly abundant, increasingly dense energy fluxes through correspondingly more complex social structures. Through alternating epochs of stability, and now exponentially increasing technology-triggered bifurcations, societies in history evolve from the low-energy and structurally relatively simple nomadic tribes of the Paleolithic to the dynamic, autonomous, and relatively complex technological nation-states of the contemporary age.

I don't think so

THE DYNAMICS OF SOCIAL EVOLUTION

Bifurcations in History

History's arrow of time does not fly smoothly. Although the historical record is always complex and frequently obscure, it gives good reasons to believe that societies, the same as biological species, do not change at all times and in small increments. Rather, the mode of change appears saltatory and intermittent, triggered by external conquests and internal discontent and by technological revolutions that change the pattern of relations between man and man and between man and nature.

The discontinuous, nonlinear mode of historical development has been noted by many historians, including Arnold Toynbee. Indeed, Toynbee's theory of "challenge and response" depicts societal change in essentially evolutionary terms. "During the disintegration of a civilization," Toynbee writes in his 1972 book *A Study of History* (p. 228), "two separate plays with different plots are being performed simultaneously side by side. While an unchanging dominant majority is perpetually rehearsing its own defeat, fresh challenges are perpetually evoking fresh creative responses from newly recruited minorities, which proclaim their own creative power by rising, each time, to the occasion." The analogy with the description of how species evolve in the theory of punctuated equilibria is evident. The "unchanging dominant majority" is the unchanging yet destabilized dominant species in the clade; the

Fig. 13. *Major Stages in the Evolution of Society*

"newly recruited minorities" are the peripheral isolates that, in "rising to the occasion," move from the periphery to invade the center.

But the relationship between societal change and biological speciation rests on more than simple analogies. The way human societies change and evolve is logical and fully expected in light of current knowledge concerning the evolution of systems far from equilibrium. Human societies, as already noted, are systems in the third state, on organizational levels far from thermodynamic equilibrium where structures can only be maintained through the reproduction of the components and the replication of the entire structure formed by their interrelations. Societies are autopoietic systems maintaining themselves in a throughput of people, resources and infrastructures, and a flow of energy, by means of autocatalytic and cross-catalytic cycles.

Societies, however, are not just autopoietic structures; they are multistable systems capable of change and transformation. Like all systems in the third state, they are subject to destabilization and bifurcation. Within certain limits the autocatalytic and cross-catalytic cycles buffer out disturbances and maintain the status quo. However, major perturbations introduced by wars and technological revolutions can destabilize the cycles and replace the overall determinism of their orderly functioning with a large degree of indeterminism. The autopoietic components—including the family as well as a large variety of institutions established and maintained by social convention—may undergo change. The nuclear family is a biological reproductive unit and thus it stays, but the context in which it functions can vary anywhere from collective child rearing by a tribe to single-parent families. More basic changes can take place among the societal structures created by convention. Social orders, economic systems, entire cultures can be discarded, transformed, or replaced. Governments can fall, new movements, ideas, and ideologies can surface. A sudden change may occur in society's autopoiesis. In terms of dynamic systems theory, society's stable attractors, which hitherto ensured orderly functioning, may turn chaotic or disappear. Society may enter a phase of subtle or catastrophic bifurcation.

A human society is a dynamic entity; even when it is stable, it fluctuates around certain norms determined by the laws, conventions, and behaviors of its members and by their relations with other societies and the environment. Like other complex dynamic systems, society can at best control its own fluctuations and maintain itself in a dynamic steady state. Stability in a society means that autopoiesis is operative: the system can ensure the reproduction and replenishment of its subsystems and its flows, including natural resources, raw materials, foodstuffs, energies, money, information—and people. Bifurcations occur when the steady state can no longer be maintained, and autopoiesis is replaced by a condition of critical instability. In this condition some or all of the flows threaten to be depleted or cut off, and all or some of the subsystems are doomed to atrophy. An unstable society cannot ensure the replenishment of its natural resources, its food and energy supplies, and its wealth, nor can it ensure the survival and reproduction of its people.

The difference between stable and unstable societies is spelled by the way the economic, social, and political systems of production, consumption, and governance operate. These societal subsystems are operated by human beings, but they are not under the full and conscious control of any individual. Rather, the production, consumption, and governance systems function according to rules of procedure created by members of society across many generations. Individuals contribute but little to the creation and change of the rules; even those in high places find their freedom of action circumscribed by the privileges and obligations of their position or office.

The sum of the rules that code the essential operations of society constitutes a basic information pool, possessed by all members of society collectively. The collective information pool is equivalent to the culture of a society, when culture is broadly defined to include the characteristic features of all human behaviors, and not merely the "high culture" of science, art, and religion.

If society's information pool (its broadly defined "culture") is up to date and operational, the production and consumption systems function adequately to maintain society in its milieu. All the essential flows are replenished; all the basic subsystems are repaired or reproduced. Society is sustainable; its people are in harmony with each other and in balance with their environment. On the other hand, society is critically unstable—and on the point of a bifurcation—if it is unable to replenish the flows and repair or reproduce its subsystems. In this unstable and nonsustainable condition, the members of society must update and transform their culture, that is, their collective information pool. They either manage this feat and attain a new and functional mode of social, economic, and political organization, or their society lapses into anarchy and may dissolve in chaos, a ready prey to more stable and powerful adversaries.

The dynamics of social evolution concern the progressive yet discontinuous development of society's collective information pool. The processes of history act on actual societies but they select cultural information pools, much as the processes of biological evolution act on actual organisms but select genetic information pools. This, then, is a deeper meaning of the term *cultural evolution*.

When destabilized by uncontrollable fluctuations, a society does not suffer extinction but is absorbed in other societies—or it transforms and renews itself. In any event, it undergoes a major phase change equivalent to a bifurcation. The historical record provides ample evidence of the occurrence of such bifurcations. As the analyses in Chapter 9 illustrate, at least three major varieties appear to have occurred with significant frequency: T-bifurcations due to the destabilizing effect of technologies; C-bifurcations induced by conflicts, and E-bifurcations due to economic and related social problems.

Theory suggests, and the detailed study of the history of any given epoch would confirm, that the nature of the new social (economic, political, cultural) order that emerges at a given time and place in the wake of a bifurcation is indeterminate with respect to the overall direction of historical development. However, the historical record also shows that the sum of such transformations in the course of time tends toward technological societies with more structural complexity and improved access, storage, and use of dense and abundant free-energy fluxes. In the long run the statistical irreversibility of technological innovation overrides the indeterminacy of individual bifurcations.

There is pattern in history as there is pattern in the evolution of order and complexity in all realms of nature. Even if outcomes are

Fig. 14. *Auto- and Cross-Catalytic Cycles in Sociocultural Systems*

Figure 14 maps the main flows in the biosphere, integrating the ecosystemic catalytic cycles of Figure 3 with the additional flows and cycles introduced by human societies.

Neglecting a large number of subsidiary flows and cycles, the basic processes are easy to grasp. Energy to drive the entire system comes from the sun (a comparatively small amount is now also derived from sources of nonsolar origin, such as nuclear and geothermal energies). Plants convert solar energy into biomass and provide food for animals. The organic wastes and decaying bodies of animals are, in turn, food for plants. Plants and animals as well as all the marine species reproduce themselves partly through natural processes in their ecosystems, partly through human intervention (plant cultivation, animal husbandry, maricultures—although the latter are as yet insignificant on the global scale). The natural life-support systems also include fossil energies (oil, coal, natural gas), the result of fossilized plant decay over aeons of time, and matter and energy sinks on land, in the water, and in the atmosphere.

On the level of human society, we note human populations constantly creating and conserving information (know-how, skills, blueprints, laws, norms, and so on). The sum of such information represents the currently operative information pool of society. It is directly accessed by people in libraries, data banks, the press, and many other ways. But much of the collective information pool is applied to produce the goods and services needed or demanded by human populations. The production structures include industrial as well as agricultural production. They operate on the basis of information, but use energy and matter inputs from the life-support systems (fossil and renewable or nuclear energies, plants, animals, marine species, and so on). The production systems also replenish the renewable part of these inputs, but if they take out more than they allow to grow back, even renewable stocks diminish over time.

People in groups and institutions monitor most of these flows; there is an information feedback loop from many parts of human activities as well as from the life-support systems. The information thus fed back is assessed by people and enters the common information pool: the broadly defined collective culture of a society. Destabilizations can occur if there is a major culture lag; that is, if information is incomplete or deficient, and if it is not acted upon in the production systems. The production systems themselves produce food and manufactured goods for human consumption, as well as capital goods for use within the production systems themselves. Services, an increasingly important part of the economic life of societies, use relatively little energy and materials; their main commodity is information. Information processed in the service sector is likewise consumed by the human populations, and is in part cycled back into the information pool.

Last but not least, it is important to note that all these complex flows and cycles (which in reality are far more complex than this figure can represent) serve to maintain human beings, enabling them to survive and to reproduce. In addition, they are also self-serving on the level of human society: the flows and cycles likewise maintain the institutions created by human populations. As long as all cycles are sustainable, the system can buffer out minor perturbations and continue to operate. But when some cycles are interrupted or collapse, major fluctuations shake the entire system, which must transform or perish.

never predetermined, it is not accidental that, given sufficient time, life should appear, and then society. It is logical, in terms of the dynamics of evolution, that on each level evolving systems should acquire greater complexity and retain more of the energy fluxes in which they are immersed. The emergence of mammals with endothermy is just as much in the logic of evolution as the emergence of technological societies. As the one is a third-state system capable of storing and using increasing amounts of increasingly dense energies on the level of individual organisms, so the other is a third-state system with equivalent capabilities on the level of groups and populations of organisms.

The adoption of increasingly energy-intensive technologies with improved (though not necessarily optimal) efficiency sets forth the evolutionary trend toward growing dynamism and autonomy in biological systems. Just as organic species evolve toward the use of greater densities of a wider variety of free-energy sources in their environment, so human societies develop to access, store, and use in greater densities larger quantities of free energy through the ongoing improvement of their technologies. As a consequence societies, the same as natural systems, tend to grow larger in size, develop more intricate relations among their diverse components, and create more massive and flexible modes of interaction among them.

The evolutionary hypothesis makes sense. History can be conceived as the evolution of systems in the third state on organizational levels typical of societies of living beings. The detailed exploration of this hypothesis should be high on the list of research priorities of social and natural scientists alike.

CONCLUDING NOTE

This review of the three great realms of evolution—the physical realm of the evolution of matter, the biological realm of the evolution of life, and the realm of history that encompasses the evolution of human society—was intended to explore and test the empirical application of the grand evolutionary synthesis outlined in Part One. As an exploration it is clearly incomplete, and as a test it may appear to be less than objective. We must remember, however, that it is not possible to test a grand evolutionary synthesis—or any conceptual scheme, for that matter—by comparing it with pristine reality. There is no immaculate perception; we do not see reality except through the spectacles of a theory. But not all spectacles allow coherent vision, not all theories, when applied to experience, can make sense of the strands of order that we intuitively believe interconnect the myriad phenomena we encounter around us. The best we can do is to prove the validity of our conceptual scheme by showing that, when we use it as a spectacle to view reality, reality appears coherent and meaningful.

The requirement for coherence and meaning underlies all efforts at our understanding of the world; more than this no concept or theory can achieve. If the grand synthesis of evolution can disclose coherence and meaning in reality, its further testing and exploration will be well worth the time and effort.

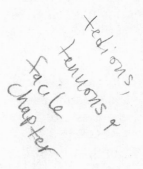

6

A Philosophical Postscript

A grand evolutionary synthesis opens wide and broad philosophical perspectives. Fundamental questions arise concerning nature, man, mind, and knowledge. Many volumes could and should be devoted to their exploration. Here just three such issues will be taken up, and merely in a preliminary and tentative manner. They concern the evolution of science, the nature and development of mind, and the likely existence of extraterrestrial intelligence.

THE EVOLUTION OF SCIENCE

Does GES apply to science—and thus (inasmuch as such a synthesis surfaces in the context of science) to itself?

The question is intriguing. Would a general theory of evolution reflect and describe its own genesis? Is the process that gives rise to the grand synthesis of the forms and processes of evolution itself an evolutionary process?

The answer is not evident. The grand synthesis of evolution refers to dynamic matter-energy systems in the empirical world; but scientific theories are conceptual systems, mental constructs created by scientists. It is true, on the other hand, that scientific theories arise through the interaction and intercommunication of scientists with each other and with "nature" within contemporary scientific communities, that is, that they emerge in the context of the interaction of some highly specific matter-energy systems with each other and with their environment.

A grand evolutionary synthesis would reflect and describe its own genesis if scientific development would indeed manifest enduring patterns, and if these patterns would prove to be isomorphic with those traced by the emergence of matter-energy systems in the empirical world. To show whether or not this is the case would require detailed studies in the history, philosophy, and sociology of science. This is beyond the scope of this postscript. But I can make a modest beginning by noting some salient points.

Since the publication in 1962 of Thomas Kuhn's *The Structure of Scientific Revolutions* it is seldom contested that scientific development follows definite patterns—regardless of whether these are exactly such as Kuhn suggested. The course of scientific innovation is not entirely random but possesses its own internal logic. Karl Popper, Imre Lakatos, Stephen Toulmin, Mario Bunge, and many other philosophers of science produced scores of learned treatises to specify this logic; they showed how scientists and scientific communities actually operate and found that maverick theorist Paul Feyerabend is off the mark when he claims that in science "anything goes."

The concept of "revolution" adds a saltatory element to the logic of scientific development. Although revolutions are sometimes contested in regard to Kuhn's original formulation (some philosophers, including Popper and Toulmin, argue that they occur more or less at all times although not in equal measure), it is generally acknowledged that scientific progress is nonlinear, marked by periodic bursts of innovation interspersing phases of relatively routine research. During periods of "normal science," fundamental tenets are not questioned; theories inspired by the underlying paradigms seem to accord with reality. Scientists are mainly conservative: they content themselves with devising additional tests for existing theories through better instrumentation and new observational techniques, and with extending the theories to as yet uninvestigated phenomena. As a result, in normal science periods, theories cover and account for more and more phenomena without fundamentally altering their conceptual structure and their underlying assumptions.

However, theories in the empirical sciences are strongly coupled to their natural environment—the specific aspect of reality that they describe and explain—and are exposed to "perturbations" from it. Environmental perturbations come in the form of new evidence (observation or instrument reading) that fails to conform to expectations and predictions flowing from the theories. Such anomalies can accumulate and cast doubt on the soundness of the theoretical core. When theories accumulate more than a critical mass of anomalies, their status changes: they no longer command the allegiance of the representative majority of scientists in the pertinent discipline. Although some scientists remain conservative and fight rear-guard action to preserve the anomaly-ridden theory, others turn revolutionary: they begin to question its most basic assumptions. Only by such revolutionary questioning could the centuries-old dominion of Newton's physics come to an end around the turn of the century: it was Einstein's fundamental insight that the mechanistic world view underlying classical physics was not to be rescued by adding equations to equations— "epicycles" to "epicycles"—to explain the anomalies. Instead, he produced the theories of special and general relativity: a fundamentally new conception of the physical universe.

Once the great revolution in physics ran its course and belief in the eternal verity of scientific truths was broken, improved techniques of observation and experimentation together with more refined analytical techniques produced an entire series of revolutions—in biology and biochemistry, in psychology, and not the least in the social sciences. Though not flattening into a continuous straight line, the path of scientific development became marked by more frequent leaps from one paradigm to another.

The basic changes denoted by "revolutions" or "paradigm shifts" not only change the basic constructs of science; they also simplify them. One of the main features of newborn theoretical conceptions is their simplicity compared with the maze of explanations which burden the theories they replace. The comparative simplicity of a construct is not to be confused with its level of comprehensibility. The concepts that make up the new theories are seldom if ever easy to grasp. As a rule they are abstract, removed from the plane of observation and common sense. For example, the formula $E = mc^2$ is simpler than the Lorentz transformation formulas by which physicists tried to salvage the Newtonian equations in view of the anomalies of black-body radiation and the constant velocity of light regardless of the motion of the observer, but it is also more abstract than anything produced by classical physics. The invariance of the Einsteinian interval in four-dimensional space-time is likewise a simple proposition, but its meaning is almost mysterious when contrasted with the Euclidean three-dimensional space and the equitably flowing one-dimensional time that frame Newton's equations of motion.

Revolutionary innovations in science order and simplify formerly cluttered and chaotic conceptual systems, but do so at the cost of greater abstraction. There was progressive simplification through abstraction in field after field of modern science; we need merely to compare the basically simple structure of Darwinian biology with the complex classification scheme of Linnaeus; the streamlined models of modern behaviorism with the esoteric theories of nineteenth-century depth psychologists, or the key conceptions of general equilibrium theory with the speculations of pre-Keynesian economists.

Yet, except for gains in simplicity and explanatory power, the outcome of scientific revolutions cannot be predicted. There is nothing predetermined about the contents of the theory that will surface following the demise of its predecessor; the only requirement is that it explain the facts explained by the previous theory plus those that are anomalous for it, and that it do so with optimum economy and simplicity. Theories consisting of entirely different concepts and based on entirely different assumptions could conceivably satisfy these requirements. According to the Mach-Duhem-Poincaré theorem, an indefinite number of theories can fit any given set of observations. Whether or not the number of candidate theories is large, it is certainly more than one. This condition provides effective choice for science in the revolutionary periods of theory innovation. Which of the several possible candidate theories is actually selected depends in large measure on such chance factors as personal insight and the moment when the hypothesis is actually presented. Timing is more important than is usually conceded: it is worth recalling that Darwin was sufficiently uneasy about the implications of his theory in nineteenth-century England that he hesitated some twenty years before presenting his ideas on the origin of species, and that Einstein succeeded in gaining adherents for his special relativity concepts only when physicists were becoming desperate for lack of a consistent and manageable theoretical framework.

It is possible—though of course unpredictable for certain—that a grand synthesis of the concepts and theories of evolution will provide the basis for the next paradigm of contemporary science. The expectation is not without foundation. There is, first of all, a distinct need for a new paradigm. The social sciences are struggling with a set of competing conceptions, and the sciences of complexity introduce ideas that are new and disturbing in view of their origin in the natural sciences. Advances in nonequilibrium thermodynamics, in cosmology, and in paleobiology create upheavals in their respective fields and lead many researchers to believe that a new scientific revolution may be just around the corner. At the same time, society at large places increasing blame on science for the havoc wrought by haphazard uses of technology and is frustrated for not receiving clear-cut answers from the scientific community.

The chaos needed to open a period of scientific revolution may be already at hand. The search for a new paradigm is likely to be weighed in favor of candidates that can integrate recent breakthroughs in important scientific fields in a coherent general conception. The successful candidate will be simple yet abstract, general yet adequate to describe and explain a wide variety of phenomena. Its coming will probably fit the overall pattern of scientific development. This pattern has been incisively described by F. S. C. Northrop. Science, in his view, progresses from an early "natural history" phase where emphasis is on fieldwork and there tend to be as many independent propositions and assumptions as there are direct observations, toward a mature, deductively formulated stage where the already gathered observations are analyzed and described in terms of the smallest possible number of primitive concepts and elementary propositions. As Northrop noted, the primitive terms of the mature theories are significantly more general than the concepts of the natural history phase. This is clearly illustrated in the evolution of the law of gravity. Galileo's law applies to all falling bodies on the surface of the earth; Newton's law applies to all bodies whether on earth or elsewhere in the universe; and Einstein's law applies to all moving bodies in space-time, even under acceleration and at velocities approaching the speed of light.

Unlike the laws of physics and of other specific scientific fields, the concepts and postulates of a grand evolutionary synthesis apply to a wide variety of disciplines in the empirical sciences. The interdisciplinary—or rather transdisciplinary—scope of GES is another important qualification in the search for a new scientific paradigm. As the Japanese scientist Kinhide Mushakoji points out, no phenomenon can be adequately known apart from the overall system of natural—and sometimes also social—realities in which it is embedded. Although individual researchers cannot cover all aspects of nature and society within the scope of their special competence, they *can* frame their research problems and assess their findings in light of general theories of wide multidisciplinary scope. A grand evolutionary synthesis allows specialized investigators to divest themselves of the blindfolds that normally accompany specialty vision and permits them to situate their particular segment of the empirical world within the relevant wider context.

GES is not unique in crossing disciplinary boundaries and connecting diverse fields of empirical investigation: almost all the sciences of complexity are multidisciplinary in scope. Ross Ashby, one of the pioneers of these sciences, once remarked that the circulation of money through banks in an economy and the circulation of blood through the kidneys in the body are essentially the same process, however odd it may seem to collapse physiology and finance. Indeed, Ashby's self-stabilizing and self-organizing model known as the "homeostat" applies equally to artificial servomechanisms and to the human brain. Norbert Wiener's cybernetics describes processes of control in animals as well as in machines; Ludwig von Bertalanffy's general system theory applies to the behavior of systems regardless of the nature of their parts or components; and the laws of contemporary thermodynamics apply to all energy-processing systems whether they are natural or artificial, living or nonliving.

The fact that a theory arches over several fields does not make it any the less valid than theories that stay within single disciplines. Nature does not observe disciplinary boundaries even if scientists do. But even scientists do so less and less today, as the relative isolation of the specialized communities of scientists gives way to intercommunication and the comparison of suppositions, methods and results. It is not surprising to encounter a growing number of general theories that embrace and integrate diverse disciplinary structures. Current trends in theory formulation conduce toward higher levels of abstraction and generality combined with greater simplicity and economy not only within specific fields but also across them; hence they lead ultimately to general theories of transdisciplinary scope. Attempts to advance grand syntheses of evolution are merely the latest, and in respect to generality the most advanced, manifestation of this trend.

The trend, noted here, toward higher levels of abstraction and generality with greater simplicity and economy across disciplinary boundaries, appears to be a secular one, enduring throughout the age of science. As long as scientists and scientific communities embrace the values they embraced since Galileo and Newton, they will be oriented toward grand syntheses of the evolutionary variety. Indeed, grand evolutionary syntheses may constitute the basic ideal of science in the long term. (For more on this point, see Appendix.)

The fact that the development of scientific theories is patterned, saltatory, unpredictable, and self-simplifying, and lifts the conceptual apparatus of science to ever-greater heights of abstraction and generality (analogously to the domains of nonequilibrium reached by evolving matter-energy systems) suggests that the development of complex interactive systems, whether they pursue their careers in the real world of matter-energy flows or in the conceptual realm of ideas, follows basically similar dynamic patterns. Very likely these patterns indicate the ultimate limits and possibilities of the evolution of complex systems in a changing environment.[1]

The development of science is itself an evolutionary process. The ideal theory would reflect and explain itself: a fully developed science of evolution would also describe the evolution of science.

THE EVOLUTION OF MIND

The phenomenon of mind is perhaps the most remarkable of all the phenomena of the lived and experienced world. Its explanation belongs to the grand tradition of philosophy—to the perennial "great questions" that each generation of thinkers answers anew . . . or despairs of answering at all.

Could this elusive issue find some elucidation in the framework of a general evolutionary hypothesis? The question itself is as intriguing as that concerning the evolution of science and is even more complex.

The first thing to remember is that we cannot investigate the human mind with the methods used to investigate the human brain, or indeed any matter-energy system in the universe. Thoughts, images, feelings, and sensations are "private": none of us has direct access to the mind of anyone else—not even of his closest friend or relative. Mind can only be investigated through introspection.

The private nature of mental phenomena and their sui generis method of investigation need not embroil us in the egocentric predicament—in the solipsist affirmation that all we can know is our own mind. We can connect our private introspections with public knowledge, building the immediately known facts and events of our consciousness into the conceptually constructed world of empirical science. Rather than assume that "my mind" is all that I can know of the world, we can assume that a scientific reconstruction of the nature of reality has validity—that it can give us as good and certain knowledge as it is humanly possible to get. While such knowledge does not have eternal validity, it does represent our most qualified guesses concerning the nature of the reality that lies somewhere beyond our mind, in public time and space. Thus we can dare to assume that the universe exists and evolves; even that in the universe systems in the third state exist and evolve. If we do make this assumption we come to the logical conclusion that we ourselves are such systems. We can then pose the more reasonable and manageable question: what is the significance of the sequence of perceptions, thoughts, and feelings that we—more precisely, that "I"—experience as mind?

The bundle of sensations that makes up my experience of mind can be most logically and parsimoniously explained as the internal description of the relations between my organism (body-cum-brain) and the environment. If my mind is a function and a manifestation of a complex nonequilibrium system, it is not unique to me, nor is it necessarily restricted to the human species. More likely it is a highly sophisticated variant of the kind of undifferentiated "feel" of the milieu that less complex systems have on the multicellular, cellular, or even subcellular levels of organization, corresponding to their sensitivity (on lower levels merely irritability) vis-à-vis their environment. Their sensitivity, in turn, is a function of the specific nature of their survival requirements. As evolution brings forth more and more complex systems, further and further from equilibrium, the requirements of survival become more stringent. They call for increasingly sophisticated capacities for distinguishing the relevant features of the environment and for searching out the appropriate sources of free energies. In the physiology of evolving biological species, the nervous system evolves from primitive ganglia into a complex brain.

If mind is indeed an internal description of relations between organism and environment, then, parallel with the evolution of the brain, mind evolves from an undifferentiated sea of primitive sensations to a locus of differentiated perceptions. As the brain becomes the organ for seeking out dense and highly specific forms of free-energy fluxes with ever more reliance on information and learning, the mind, being the internal read-out of the operations of the brain, becomes the means for orienting the organism with ever-greater refinement toward ever-greater autonomy in its surroundings.

The human mind, however, is not just the subjective side of a two-sided survival mechanism. The mind, as introspection reveals, is also the seat of abstract thought, feeling, imagination, and value. I not only sense the world, I also interpret my sensations. Like presumably all human beings, I have consciousness. I am aware of having sensations and, on successively higher levels of abstraction, I am aware of being aware of having sensations. Ultimately I, like other members of the human species, learn to abstract from immediate sensations in ways that lesser species cannot, and can come to deal with pure *forms* of thought. These include scientific and mathematical concepts, aesthetic constructions, and the abstract meaning of words and concepts. Consciousness is not a mysterious transcendental trait: it is the capacity for internally describing the internal description of the perceived and conceived environment.[2]

Neurophysiologists find that consciousness in human subjects is associated with the functioning of the frontal lobes of the neocortex. As these regions were the last to evolve—perhaps only about 200,000 to 250,000 years ago—consciousness as we know it may have been experienced only by a handful of hominid species, and for the last 30,000 years only by *sapiens*. This, however, does not mean that other species, and in fact all systems in the third state, would not have internal descriptions of their relations with the environment. The lack of a large neocortex means only that they cannot analyze these descriptions on levels of precision and abstraction that human beings can.

A system capable of both sensing its environment and analyzing the description of its sensations is a highly sophisticated entity. It knows its milieu, and knows that it is knowing it. It can identify sets of sensory perceptions with objects and events, and establish relations and connections among them. It can come to believe that it knows not only its own stream of sensations but the external world itself. Such knowledge is, of course, hypothetical. It is testable, however, since it is prone to error. The possibility of error is important: it is the key not only to the validity of knowledge but also to its improvement. Error is the price paid for learning. Were living systems to persist in basic errors, they would soon be weeded out by natural selection. In humans such selection would operate first of all in the competition for essential sources of free energy (air, water, and food) and then in the equally crucial competition for information (knowledge, skills, social orientation, etc.).

Species that survive do not persist in basic errors but learn to correct them. The new solutions may likewise contain errors that come to light subsequently. Thus an endless vista is opened for learning. And learning, being empirical rather than genetic, is relatively rapid: it takes place in the lifetime of individuals, not of species.

Learning leads to the emergence of differences between members of the same species and creates true individuals. The brain is known to develop much as the embryo develops: by progressive differentiation among groups of cells. The process is not determined directly by the genes but indirectly by the combined effect of genes and signals from cell groups that activate genes: it is epigenetic rather than genetic. Just as identical twins are never truly identical, already because of the differentiation of the epigenetic development of their physiology, so the brains of two individuals, even if they could be exposed to the same set of stimuli, could never be identical owing to the fact that different neuronal groups would be activated by the stimuli.

Individually differentiated brains are the external, observer-oriented dimension of the individually differentiated minds presented "internally" to each human being. As the brain maps incoming stimuli in a variety of ways by sorting them according to various, uniquely differentiated "maps," the mind perceives and cognizes the environing world in various, individually unique ways. As the environment changes, so do the multiple categories of perception in the mind and the multiple mappings in the brain. Unique individuals cope with the world in unique ways. Thus, like all systems in the third state, humans have a basic "divergence property." Because they are highly evolved systems with complex and differentiated brains, the divergent pathways of their development lead to individuals who are highly differentiated in their psychology, and not only in their physiology.

But we should not separate the evolution of mind from the evolution of society: the two take place simultaneously and in close relation. Because the human brain is capable of multiple mappings, and the mind of empirical learning, human societies are capable of rapid evolution. They move from survival-oriented hunting-gathering tribes and primitive agrarian communities to so-called civilized societies where culture plays a dominant role and survival is assured by an ever smaller segment of the population in an ever-shorter period of time. The individual becomes increasingly free to learn: to explore the world, liberated from the survival chores of finding food, clothing, and shelter. (The time required for sleep seems not to have been reduced—and the time taken up by courtship and mating seems actually to have increased.)

The reduction of the segment of the population that takes care of basic survival needs is a historical phenomenon. As the social system becomes more dynamic, while the biological requirements of its human population remain constant, more and more of the dynamic capability of society is channeled into activities that have little to do with physical survival. The process has been known to social scientists for centuries. Already in 1691 the British economist William Petty wrote that "as Trade and the Curious Arts increase; so the Trade of Husbandry will decrease." In 1938 the Australian economist Colin Clark divided the economy into three sectors, agriculture, manufacturing, and services, and noted that each of the sectors flowered in turn. This process holds good today. In the United States the service sector had outgrown the previously dominant manufacturing sector already in 1960. Japan,

the society that is perhaps the furthest along its historical trajectory, no longer has a full-time agricultural work force. The fastest-
growing sector in most of the European economies is the one
concerned with information processing and related services.

In its irreversible development technology not merely saves
labor; it detaches it from the survival chores and functions of
people. It shifts the bulk of the work force from hunting, fishing,
and gathering food, and later from growing it, to building abodes,
drawing boundaries, administering lands, producing and storing
goods, performing services, and finally to the pursuits of reflecting
on the origin and the destiny of things, of searching for beauty,
harmony, and meaning in ever more diverse ways.

As the needs of survival become filled in society, people experience other needs, including the "higher" needs for aesthetic
enjoyment, intellectual satisfaction, and ultimate meaning. And as
people pursue the satisfaction of these needs, society acquires a
cultural superstructure, connected with, but no longer subservient
to, the feedbacks and catalytic cycles that maintain a social system
in its environment.

The human mind, triggering the evolution of ever more technologically advanced societies, frees itself from the sphere of survival
and creates the sphere of culture. If it now succeeds in mastering
the increasingly automated technologies of postindustrial societies,
it will have the opportunity to evolve still more varied cultural
pursuits, still further removed from the chores of physical survival.

The mind does not evolve in a vacuum, nor indeed does it evolve
in the isolated individual. Mind and culture co-evolve with technology and society: a technologically sophisticated society is at the
same time the product of the evolving mind and its generating
environment.

From vulnerability to changes in the environment—to irritability
and responsiveness to finer shades of change—to differentiated
perception and selective behavior that not merely responds but
creates and initiates, mind evolves as the subjective dimension of
the objective survival functions of complex nonequilibrium systems. Freed by technological innovation from time-consuming
survival chores, and driven by the need to find outlets for its
creative energies and impulses, the learning mind creates the world
of culture. The human mind evolves as technological society

evolves, and they both evolve as systems in the third state do in nature: toward greater complexity and autonomy in interaction with the environment.

A NOTE ON EXTRATERRESTRIAL INTELLIGENCE

The search for life, especially intelligent life, outside the confines of our home planet has always fascinated poets and scientists; in recent years it has motivated major research efforts. Alas, these efforts have not brought positive results. But neither have they brought disproof of the existence of intelligent beings elsewhere in the universe. While the search continues, we can speculate on the probabilities and assess the chances that we may one day come in contact with highly evolved extraterrestrial beings.

Our point of departure is the hypothesis of the universality of the laws and processes of nature. If evolution occurred on earth, it would occur elsewhere in the cosmos under similar conditions. To deny this violates the most basic assumptions of contemporary science—and all our hypotheses about the nature of the world that surrounds us. GES postulates that whenever certain conditions are met, certain processes will occur, including the formation of systems in the third state. It makes not the least difference whether the conditions are met *in vivo* or *in vitro,* or whether they are met on the surface of planet Earth or on Alpha Centauri.

As already noted, the human traits that differentiate our species are not necessarily unique in the cosmos. They are evolutionary responses to the challenges that await open systems in the third state as they explore the higher levels of nonequilibrium in the course of their evolution. Characteristics as unpredictable as those of our species may appear here and there; hominoid creatures endowed with intelligence may walk the surface of other planets.

This assumption becomes entirely reasonable if we assume that the information available to astronomers today concerning the dimensions of the observable universe is basically correct. Under this assumption we get a significant probability that life exists elsewhere in the cosmos. The probability of *intelligent* life is much smaller, but it is by no means insignificant. We need merely to recall the equation proposed by Frank Drake (see note 6 for

Chapter 3). He suggests that we take the rate at which stars form, multiply it by the fraction of stars with planets, multiply this by the fraction of the average number of planets physically capable of supporting life, multiply the result further by the fraction of planets that actually give rise to life, and further multiply by the fraction of life-supporting planets that generate intelligence. Given some 200 billion stars in the Milky Way, and the fact that perhaps 5 percent of them emit light in the range required for life—and that about half of these may have planets capable of supporting some form of life—as many as 5 billion biospheres could exist in our galaxy alone. Of these, a small but not negligible number may have produced, or will produce in the future, intelligent forms of life.

The odds decrease if we follow Drake further in his calculations. He requires that we multiply the number of life-supporting planets that generate intelligence by the fraction of intelligent species that have the technology as well as the motivation to communicate— and multiply again by the average life expectancy of the motivated technological civilizations. It is this last factor that may give trouble. We have no difficulty in believing that a large fraction of species that have the intelligence to evolve technology actually do so: the advent of technological society, GES claims, is not a random but a lawlike factor in the evolution of systems on the level of complex organic species. On the other hand, we can see no guarantees that a technological society, once evolved, will also survive. The gamble of evolution finds its highest expression in a society that taps the atom for energy and manipulates the movement of electrons for information, communication, and control, and does so by means of relatively simple and immature societal structures and mechanisms. A technological society, especially if it is of recent origin, could well self-destruct and take with it most or all of its biosphere.

Could it be that the reason we have been unable to make contact with extraterrestrial civilizations is that their life expectancy is extremely short? This answer cannot be proven, but it also cannot be ruled out. Its probability is enhanced by the problems we already experience in controlling our own technological prowess on earth. Perhaps, the greatest hurdle is the one that now awaits us: to evolve the societal structures that are sufficiently mature to cope with the technological genius of their members. If so, this is all the more reason for us to concern ourselves with evolution on our own planet. Whatever has befallen the extraterrestrial civilizations that most likely evolved in the depth of cosmic space, it would be more than a pity if human civilization came to a premature end. Our past evolution was not an accident of nature; it is now up to us to make sure that our future evolution does not turn into an accident of human folly.

Part Three

The Mastery of Evolution

7

Intervention in Evolution

The unfolding of the evolutionary process in the three great realms of matter, life, and society raises a crucial question. It is this: are the highly complex systems that emerge in each realm truly enduring?

As we have seen, evolution produces comparative simplicity as it moves to a higher level of organization, but in time simplicity gives way to complexity as third-state systems pursue their careers in interaction with a changing environment. On each level of organization, systems reach some functional limit of complexity beyond which further complexification would bring instability. The atoms of the elements, beyond a certain level of complexity (measured by atomic weight and number) become unstable. Complex molecular aggregates are subject to dissolution and decay. Complex species, especially if highly specialized, are prone to extinction. The blue-green algae are all but immortal; *Homo,* the most complex of the higher mammals, is the prey of the simplest of viruses. The kinship-based hunting-gathering tribe is practically indestructible, capable of persistence as long as there are no major changes in its natural and societal environment; a more complex technological society is vulnerable to accidents and to sabotage, to external attack and to internal value change. The fact of the matter is that the evolution of complex systems involves a gamble: the sacrifice of basic structural stability for sophisticated control.

Homo is the most complex system in the biosphere. Is he now doomed to extinction?

The danger to our species comes in the form of instabilities in technological societies. Because our brains have evolved sufficiently to permit symbolic communication and joint planning, we could evolve societies based on subtle strands of interrelations

127

with multiple roles and complex divisions of labor. Because the evolutionary logic favors the emergence of systems with growing utilization of free energies, we tend to create, through the many twists and turns of history, dynamic supertechnological societies. Endowed with an as yet immature controlling structure, our societies could release enormous quantities of energy and inflict possibly irreparable harm to human populations and their life-sustaining environment.

Can *Homo* survive technological societies? Is a species capable of tapping the energy of the atom and mastering the intricacies of electronics also capable of long-term persistence? This is by no means certain. It is not encouraging that we have not succeeded in contacting extraterrestrial civilizations, although we have good reasons to believe in the existence of intelligent species on planets within communication range. It is worrying that we are unable to control the arms race, to clean up dangerous technologies, and to halt the degradation of the environment.

But even if rare, the survival of complex species need not be foreclosed. It is possible, in principle, to master the evolutionary processes of high-energy technological societies by purposeful action based on a sound knowledge of socio-developmental dynamics. The crucial question is not one of principle but of practice. Will *Homo* make use of his capacities for knowledge and action to steer the evolution of technological societies within the limits of survival?

PREDICTABILITY VERSUS CONTROL

If human beings are to steer the evolution of societies they must be able to control the processes of its unfolding. But can such control be truly exercised? If we say that society is a system in the third state, we must admit that its evolution is inherently unpredictable. Does this not mean that it is also inherently uncontrollable?

In the evolutionary view of history, determinism alternates with indeterminism, order with chaos. During phases of deterministic order, society is predictable, at least in principle: if we know enough of the elements that make up a society, of the forces that govern it, and of the forces that act upon it from its environment, we can also foretell within some limit of precision how society will behave, that is, what its approximate state or condition will be in the future. However, during a phase change, determinism vanishes and a knowledge of the elements and of the forces acting in and on society does not suffice to foretell its future behavior. Multiple trajectories become available, and the observer is intrinsically incapable of saying which of them will be adopted.

Human societies, like all systems in the third state, evolve through relatively rapid phase changes. Thus history is full of surprises. Are we, then, forever incapable of mastering the evolution of our societies—and thus our destinies?

The assumption that a process that is unpredictable is also uncontrollable is often made, but it is false. Unpredictability means only that an external observer, even if he controls certain parameters of the system, is unable to decide which of several alternative states will be realized in the system. It does not mean that an element *in* the system would be unable to critically influence the choice of its future states.

We must distinguish between predicting from the outside and manipulating from the inside if we are to grasp the possibilities of mastering the course of social evolution. While it is true that a historian living today could not predict with assurance the outcome of a process of societal bifurcation—as indeed historians were unable to predict the outcome of major technological and sociopolitical revolutions in the past—it is false that an activist working within society could not consciously influence the outcome to better conform to his or her goals and ideals. If an activist acts with a sound knowledge of the dynamics of social evolution and intervenes at the right place, at the right time and in the right way, he or she can create that tiny but crucial internal fluctuation that the nondeterministic and nonlinear dynamics of an otherwise random process of bifurcation could amplify into society's dominant operating mode. The goals and ideals projected by the activist could become the attractors of society's next systemic state, pulling it out of chaos and onto the next plateau of order.

The distinction between unpredictability and uncontrollability can be made clear by considering the behavior of different kinds of systems. If we take a simple mechanism such as a clock, we can get full predictability in principle: if we know the initial state of the system (the tension of the spring, the rate of its unwinding, and the transfer of force within the parts), we can also foretell any of its subsequent states, including the position of the hands while the clock is still in motion and the position of the hands when the clock has finally wound down. (Pierre Laplace believed that the entire universe, conceived in Newtonian mechanistic terms, was a clockwork of this kind, permitting full predictability for a "demon" that completely knew its state at any given time.) If we then take an electric clock connected to an outside power supply, we still get full predictability provided that we know the rate at which the current is passing into the system from the power source and the length of time that it does so. We can now vary the workings of the clock by increasing or decreasing the current, or interrupting it altogether. Knowing the input parameter as well as the clock's mechanism, we can still predict the position of the hands at any given time in the future. But if we take a mechanism that has internal processes that decide which of several alternative states it will occupy, and specify that these processes are locked up in a "black box" that cannot be opened, then we can vary the system's power supply as we like and we shall still not know which alternative state will be chosen by the system. Such a system—be it an organism, a society, or an artificial servomechanism whose codes we do not know—is not determined by its initial conditions, nor by its environmental parameters. It is *self*-determined to some significant degree. In virtue of such self-determination its behavior is essentially unpredictable by the outsider—but it is not uncontrollable by the decision codes of the system. Given identical initial conditions, and identical variations in the environmental parameters, two such systems will enter on divergent trajectories, depending merely on differences between their internal dynamics. If these dynamics are not fully deterministic (they could have random or chaotic features), the behavior of the self-determined system, unlike that of the clockwork, is unpredictable from the outside. But it is not, by that token, uncontrollable from the inside.

Society is a self-determined system of this kind. Its evolution cannot be predicted, but it can be controlled. During a critical phase change, control is not in the form of a rigid set of deterministic laws or rules that the system "obeys." Rather, it is in the form of dynamic inputs at precise points in the system, at precise phases of its transformation. The evolution of society can be controlled by humans who act within it—provided that they act the right way, at the right place, and at the right time.

WARRANT FOR INTERVENTION

We should not take intervention in social evolution lightly, despite the vulnerability of technological societies and the dangers they pose to human welfare and survival. Is intervention in an evolutionary process, *any* evolutionary process, warranted?

The answer should be a clear cut yes, when it comes to the evolution of *human* society. We cannot, and perhaps should not, interfere with the unfolding of evolution in the realms of nature. But when it comes to evolution in the realms of history, the case is different. Here *we* are the actors, and it is *our* future that is at stake. Unless we dare interfere with the coding of the chromosomes that define the information pool of our species to create a mutant human being—an attempt that is as dangerous as it is foolhardy—the only way we can guide our destiny on this planet is to steer the processes of social change and transformation.

Intervention in the processes of contemporary social change is of vital importance. In the absence of conscious intervention, the direction of evolution through any phase change is largely undetermined. Systems in the third state incorporate their past in their present, but they do not incorporate their future. They possess the future only in the form of multiple possibilities of transformation, of multiple trajectories unfolding through sequences of individually indeterminate bifurcations.

Applied to society, this means that even if there is a statistical irreversibility in the full sweep of historical development, any given trajectory selected by a social system can be consistent with, or else contrary to, the historical trend. It is by no means a coincidence that practically all the major revolutions of the twentieth century fall into the category of historical events whose outcomes were not, and probably could not be, predicted at the time. Whether we take the events in Russia, Germany, China, Cuba, Iran, or Central America, we find that the same dynamic pattern repeats in local variations. There is a destabilized regime confronted with various alternative movements; when the regime falls, one among the several previously suppressed and peripheral movements suddenly gains power. Unless there is a massive military intervention from the outside, the choice among them appears to be random, determined only by the interplay of minor fluctuations within the domestic social structure.

In natural systems, bifurcations are always and necessarily random: they do not have conscious members capable of planning and foresighted action. Human societies do have members endowed with such capacities, and if their members would begin to exercise them, social change in contemporary societies would not remain largely indeterminate. Acting on plans and strategies based on an essentially correct understanding of the processes of evolution could bias society's bifurcation, loading the dice in favor of consciously selected outcomes.

There is never any point in insisting on the impossible. "Ought" said the philosopher Kant, always implies "can." But if so, then there *is* a point in insisting on intervention in the evolution of contemporary societies. This process *can* be purposively steered—and on the success of such steering depends the future of humanity. Therefore we *ought* to intervene in the evolution of our societies, and do so to the best of our knowledge and our ability.

8

Evolution in Our Hands

The evolution of contemporary societies can be steered. Doing so is warranted in view of the dangers of uncontrolled bifurcations. We *can* select favorable outcomes, and we *should* select them. But how do we know which outcomes are favorable?

This question is of overwhelming importance. Even if we cannot decide it fully, we must try to sketch out an answer. Change in contemporary societies will not wait until we have crossed all the *t*'s and dotted all the *i*'s. In great outline, if not in fine detail, we can orient ourselves already.

WHERE DO WE GO FROM HERE? THE LARGE-SCALE MAP

If we are to chart the horizons of social change in our day and age and decide what future developments are truly good and desirable, we need a historical vision, embedded in the still broader framework of the evolutionary vision. We need to know where the current transformations that move societies along the vast though jagged and discontinuous sweep of historical development fit into the general pattern; we need to know how far we have come, and how far we can go. This calls for a large-scale map, a bird's-eye view from a high altitude. Only such an altitude can give us the necessary orientation; only a large-scale map can reveal the basic pattern. There will be time and opportunity to fill in the details, add specifications, and draw smaller-scale maps at lower altitudes. First we must ascend to the level of a grand evolutionary synthesis and get the large picture—the picture of the forest, and not only of this or that clump of trees.

133

The Evolutionary Switching Scenario

History, in the perspective of GES, is the record of the evolution of human sociocultural systems. In the span of recorded history, from the dawn of the Neolithic to the present, a wide variety of sociocultural systems have made their appearance, and, while many have transformed into historically newer systems, many types of systems still persist. The range of societal types stretches from the still surviving but now rapidly disappearing Stone Age hunters and gatherers here and there in Asia, Oceania, Australia, Africa, and Latin America to the techno-industrial societies of Europe, North America, and East Asia. The wave of societal transformations exhibits the overall directionality of history, moving from the small, comparatively less dynamic, less autonomous and simple, to the large-scale, more complex, more dynamic and autonomous social system, impelled by irreversible technological innovations and the structural changes catalyzed by them.

But the wide spectrum of societal types in the contemporary world does not add up to a well-balanced and smoothly functioning system. There are traditional societies barely out of the agrarian-pastoral phase, societies just entering the phase of the first industrial revolution, and societies that are already on the threshold of the postindustrial age. The presence of societies at different evolutionary stages means the coexistence of different evolutionary time frames. Yet all societies, front-runners and laggards alike, are embedded in a tightening web of increasing interaction and interdependence. The growing tempo of change in the contemporary world forces all societies to change and to adapt. Those that are imperfectly and insufficiently evolved need to change more; and it is not impossible that some of the required changes should prove to be in the nature of catastrophic bifurcations.

Since the evolution of societies is not a unidimensional progression tending toward one specific type of society, but an open-ended process in which merely the increases of autonomy, of dynamism, of organizational levels, and of structural complexities are the shared features, it is misleading to think of backward societies as "catching up" to any type of society already on the scene. Instead of ranging societies along a single track, like coaches on a railway line, we should think of branching trajectories, where each self-propelled vehicle moves along its own route in a shared general direction. We should perceive that each vehicle seeks autonomy and greater power over its own destiny, but perceive, too, that all vehicles enter an increasingly interconnected network of rails. As the powered vehicles move along the interacting switches toward their individual yet shared destinations, some are more prone to derailment than others: the interconnections among the switches create sudden turns and call for skill and control on the part of the engineers.

Such images are helpful in orienting thinking in complex situations. If we are to develop a reasonably adequate map of the historical condition of humanity, we should think in terms of images of branching tracks and self-propelled vehicles, powered by technology and buffeted by strands of interdependence. We should distinguish between those that have good guidance systems and greater autonomy and thus enjoy a smoother ride, and others who face major jolts and upsets, and require complete overhauls.

This "evolutionary switching scenario" is no doubt primitive, but less so than the classical "railroad scenario" still current today. For we cannot disregard the fact that societies propel themselves along branching evolutionary trajectories and that they require skill and control to negotiate the switches. In the complex economic and political environment of the late twentieth century, different societies are exposed to change in the international economic, political, and social environment to different degrees. We need to perceive differences in levels of vulnerability to change, and thus in the ability of societies to adapt, transform, and develop.

Specialist and Generalist Societies

If we are to perceive differences in levels of vulnerability in contemporary societies, we should turn to the biologically proven concepts of specialist and generalist. As noted in Chapter 4, in the evolution of organic species, the specialists are highly vulnerable to change in the environment and are thus forced to speciate relatively often. Generalist species, on the other hand, can adapt to a wider range of environmental fluctuations without risking extinction. But *specialist* and *generalist* are concepts derived from macroevolutionary theory. How, precisely, do we define them in the context of human society?

The concept of generalist and specialist can be best grasped in terms of the standard definitions of *core* (or *center*) and *periphery* in international development theory. Core countries are usually defined as having a broad and differentiated economic structure with considerable capital intensity and high technology. At the periphery, on the other hand, are countries with a narrow economic base and a high share of variable cost sectors, especially labor, joined with traditional activities. According to the *dependencia* theory popular in Latin America, the countries of the periphery become dependent on outside forces and conditions as they specialize in the demands of the internationally dominant core countries.

When the problematic geographic dimension of core and periphery is disregarded and the functional elements are emphasized, we obtain an equivalence in regard to sensitivity to change between generalist species and core countries on the one hand, and specialist species and countries at the periphery on the other. Generalist species, the same as core countries, have resilient structures with significant reliance on endogenous capabilities. Their high level of differentiation enables them to adapt to a large scale of variation in the environment; they are systems with multiple levels of stability and can switch relatively smoothly from one steady state to another. Specialist species and peripheral countries have much less differentiation and diversity; they are at the mercy of their current niche in the external environment. Their actual steady states cannot be readily replaced; such replacement would call for a thorough revision of all their operative structures, that is, for a bifurcation of the entire system.

In today's international system, the peripheral specialists greatly outnumber the core generalists. The vast majority of the over 180 nation-states that claim sovereign status are highly specialized and in fact considerably less than sovereign. They are forced into narrow niches within world production systems, world markets, and world politics. Only societies that command a high level of technology (or a high level of control and discipline) as well as the people and the resources of entire continents or subcontinents—like the United States, the Soviet Union, the People's Republic of

China, and Australia—conserve a significant degree of generalist self-sufficiency. Most others, whether solvent like Kuwait or destitute like Chad, are true specialists. Their niche may consist of one or at the most a few specific export items (such as oil, bauxite, copper, some other minerals and metals, certain agricultural products, and perhaps some manufactures) or a cheap labor force. In some cases the specialty niche is simply an attractive climate and natural beauty, favoring tourism, or a strategic geographic location qualifying the country for special treatment by a major military power.

All specialty niches in today's world are highly sensitive to change. If the price of the exportable natural resource drops, or if the market for it shrinks, export revenues drop—and if cheaper synthetic substitutes are found, the revenues dry up altogether. If automated technologies reduce or eliminate the need for a certain kind of labor force, the advantages of a large and cheap labor pool vanish. Strategic positions can likewise shift in consequence of new developments in weapons technologies, while income from tourism fluctuates with fads and fashion in travel as well as with the vagaries of international exchange rates. Since the majority of the over 180 nation-states in today's world are specialists, in coming years the evolutionary dynamic of social bifurcations is likely to produce national crises at an accelerated pace.

The National States / Global Flows Gap

The way beyond crises for specialist societies is to undertake the next step in their evolution, and this step is the acceleration of transnational convergence.

A basic principle of evolution, convergence applies in all its realms, from the physical through the biological to the social. When systems in a milieu evolve interactions that penetrate beyond their boundaries, their structure-maintaining catalytic cycles interact and, in time, begin to interlock. They evolve into hypercycles that herald the emergence of a system on the next level of organization, formed by the convergence of the component systems. In the case of human society, this means that when the flows produced by a society—flows of people, information, energy, goods and manufactures, etc.—transcend its national boundaries, they interact with the flows produced by other societies. Interaction creates interdependence, or the domination of the weak by the strong. If the process is to unfold with fairness and benefit to all, interdependence would have to evolve symmetrically and conduce to collective autonomy. Collective autonomy among societies would signify that the catalytic cycles that regulate the transborder flows have coalesced into transnational hypercycles. They would then maintain the structure and regulate the functions of a new, transnational community formed by interacting, interdependent, and now collectively autonomous partner countries.

In today's world, only a few societies have developed adequate levels of autonomy. The contemporary flows of money, raw materials, people, food, manufactures, technologies, raw data, and information are yet to form equitable hypercycles. Lacking transnational mechanisms of regulation and control, they are prey to selfish motivations and interests. They benefit the strong and debilitate the weak. They are especially threatening to vulnerable specialists among contemporary societies. Although a few specialist economies—such as Singapore, Hong Kong, South Korea, and Taiwan, among others—manage to find profitable niches for themselves, the majority of the specialists—that is, the some 120 Third World countries that have neither large supplies of valuable natural resources nor command an evolved technological infrastructure— find themselves in an increasingly untenable situation. The contemporary transnational flows favor generalist societies with a large resource base and those few specialists that can meet current demands and requirements. They produce highly asymmetrical forms of interdependence and fail to ensure mutual interests and mutual benefits. As yet, there is no transnational order worthy of the name. We live not in a global village, but in national villages locked into a global flux.

In order to cope with their vulnerability to sudden and essentially unforeseeable change, the great majority of contemporary nation-states—especially the traditional and resource-poor specialists among them—would have to achieve some form of integration among themselves. It would be naive to expect that such integration could already occur on a global level. The shift from the national to the global level of social organization is not likely to be accomplished in one fell swoop; a global state as an integrated community of nations awaits a future evolutionary epoch. On the other hand, the more modest shift from the national to the regional level may be more realistic. It would set forth a historical progression that has resulted in vast empires, and later in modern nation-states. The sequential interlocking of transsocietal catalytic cycles in multilevel hypercycles has produced the world of today, and if allowed to continue will also produce the world of tomorrow.

But the process of convergence among insistently sovereign nation-states is lagging dangerously. Despite transnational flows, in most regions convergence has not penetrated significantly beyond the national level. Villages and rural areas are organized on their own level as well as coordinated within regional states or provinces; these in turn are organized on their own intermediate levels and are also integrated in nation-states. On national levels there is a dense system of organization, with ministries and departments regulating (or at least seeking to regulate) almost all dimension in the life of contemporary societies.

Above the national level, however, coordination and integration soon lapse into ad hoc ties or chaos. Further progress in the transnational dimensions is blocked by the myth of the sovereign nation-state. Nation-states do not hold themselves accountable to any higher authority and claim full sovereignty for themselves in regard to their people, their territory, and their natural resources. But the processes of social evolution do not stop when national governments decree themselves sovereign. Transnational flows continue to intensify and to interact, and they create interdependence and vulnerability among unequal partners.

On first sight this analysis appears unduly pessimistic. After all, an entire plethora of international organizations has come into being since the end of World War II. Surely such bodies control and regulate some aspects of the transnational flows in the joint interests of all. Unfortunately, a deeper analysis dispels facile hopes attached to the work of international organizations. International organizations are just that: they are *inter-national*, that is, they operate between, and in the perceived interests of, contemporary nation-states. Their powers of decision making are strictly curtailed by the fact that their members declare themselves sovereign and view the organizations as forums for the promotion of their own national interests. International bodies are effective if the member states can use them to further their own purposes, and they lapse into mere bureaucracies if they cannot. Today's international organizations are tools for furthering national interests rather than effective instruments for the articulation and implementation of inter-nationally congruent and convergent goals and designs.

International organizations are constitutionally constrained to serve their nation-state masters, and multinational businesses, while more autonomous and often also more powerful, are committed to their own corporate goals and interests. They all interact with or create transnational and global flows, but none is effective in organizing transnational hypercycles to sustain all people and states with some degree of autonomy and stability.

There are no signs in today's world that nation-states would be ready to surrender any element of their power. Indeed, neo-nationalism is on the rise. The more national governments are frustrated by problems that are intractable on the national level, the more they take recourse to national protectionism and national security based on armaments that make other nations less secure. The sacrosanct nature of national sovereignty is emphasized in almost all parts of the world and in all varieties of economic and political systems. In the First World of industrialized nations, the welfare state prompts an expansion of the public sector and impedes structural adjustments that would be otherwise available to liberal free market societies. The Second World of socialist countries, caught in the race between public expectations and the limitations of a planned economy, liberalizes some aspects of economic activity but reinforces the supervisory role of the state both to avoid going too far on the capitalist road and to safeguard national security in a hostile international environment. In the Third World, national elites reinforce state structures in continued efforts at nation-building—the building of national unity and national economy, as well as national culture and identity—in a climate that becomes increasingly complex and uncertain, and unfavorable to development.

A few societies—Albania, Burma, and Tanzania, among others—attempted to close themselves off from the world environment to practice some form of national autarky. They did not fare well. The most successful among contemporary states were precisely those that did not hesitate to open up to international and global flows: Japan, the newly industrialized countries of Southeast Asia, and now China.

But not even the most open societies relax their hold on national sovereignty. Practically all of today's over 180 nation-states engage in systematic attempts to block the evolutionary process of transnational convergence. The result is the progressive loss of control by national governments, the progressive ungovernability of national societies, an exponential growth of national insecurity, and a greatly increased risk of breakdown in the now-obsolete institutions of the international system.

HOW DO WE GET THERE?: PRACTICAL GOALS

System-Level Goals

The specific answer to the challenge of contemporary social evolution varies from society to society. On the whole it involves a basic transformation for those societies that occupy specialized niches in the current, rapidly changing international system. Specialized societies need to master transnational flows through coordinated and cooperative regional structures. This means a change not merely in economic policy and international finance. It means the development of an atmosphere of mutual trust within which selected cooperative projects can be successfully implemented; it means phasing out narrow, short-term, and self-centered economic and political strategies antithetical to long-term cooperation with neighbors and partners in a regional community.

One cannot transform a sovereign nation-state into a dependable partner in a regional system without fundamentally altering the character of the entire society. Such alteration is the most urgent for societies on the periphery, already destabilized by the chaotic fluctuations and inequitable effects of global flows. These are the underdeveloped, traditional, or highly specialized socioeconomic systems. These systems, of great vulnerability, could soon find themselves faced with major crises signaling the onset of a catastrophic bifurcation. For specialists on the periphery the creation of transnational associations or communities capable of mitigating levels of dependence and achieving the required minimum of collective self-reliance is a sine qua non of persistence. For larger, more generalist societies at the center—the United States, the Soviet Union, China, Japan, a group of western European countries, and Australia—the challenge is less drastic. These relatively autonomous societies have greater resilience when faced with a changing environment; the change required of them is not in the nature of a catastrophic bifurcation but of farsighted adaptation. One aspect of such adaptation is to develop outward- and forward-looking policies. Generalist societies would have to become catalysts of transnational structures among peripheral specialists in the less developed parts of the world, mainly in Africa, Asia, and Latin America.

We can make a simple thought experiment and map out the nature of the societies that would result if the current wave of social bifurcations were to be successfully completed. Suppose that we are in the year 2000 and no nuclear nightmare has been visited on humanity. Suppose, also, that the impending crises of the 1980s and the 1990s have been successfully negotiated. In viewing the international system "from above," we find a transnational order of regional rather than global dimensions. In place of societies that are de facto vulnerable and dependent even if de juro sovereign and independent, there are associations of states that enjoy a significant level of collective self-reliance and autonomy. In place of large, relatively self-reliant powers intent only on furthering their own economic and political designs by keeping smaller actors on a string and competitors at each other's throats, we have cooperating partners within an emerging system of individually and collectively generalist societies. The hypercycles capable of maintaining all nations and peoples at a satisfactory level of dynamic stability have begun to operate. Nation-states converge effectively among themselves, forming regional associations among themselves, or furthering such associations as equitable partners.

Viewed "from below," we witness a basic transformation in the tenor of life in turn-of-the-century societies. The uncertainty inspired by fear of powerful states that are adversaries and could turn into enemies is allayed. The confidence and solidarity that accompany partners in mutually beneficial cooperative ventures have spread. Transnational associations in the public as well as in the private sector take into account each region's long-term economic and security interests, cultural values, and developmental priorities.

The over 180 nation-states of the late twentieth century have lost some of their (anyway largely fictitious) sovereignty, but did not lose their national identity. Functional cooperation within a higher-level structure does not entail loss of identity: as villages maintain their identity within regions, regions within states, and states within federated nation-states, so nations maintain their identity within new and flexible transnational structures that integrate vulnerable specialist states within a region's collectively generalist community. The fact that a nation would assume specialized functions within a regional community is no more threatening to its survival as a distinct entity than the participation of a cell in a multicellular organism is threatening to *its* survival in the body.

But let us return to the present. The need for countries at the periphery to shift their governance and organization to the collective level of an autonomous region is imperative. It is very likely the sole strategy capable of assuring a nonviolent transition to the next evolutionary stage. Regional systems could be self-reliant generalists if their members would converge their economic, financial, and security functions and capabilities within them. The principle is simple: if the whole system formed by the parts is dynamically stable, the subsystems that form the system enjoy a stable environment within which to exist—or to change. The principle applies within nations as well as between them. For example, the Kansas Corn Belt is specialized within the U.S. economy, and the Ruhr industrial region is likewise specialized within the German economy, but if the U.S. and the German economies are self-reliant and capable of coping with a wide range of changes in the international environment, the Kansas and the Ruhr subsystems are cushioned and protected. Should they need to change or transform, the changes and transformations will be not life-or-death challenges but controlled adaptations within an established framework. The same is true internationally. The transformation of a country such as Togo within a functioning West African community, and of a state such as Honduras within a community of Central American states, could be cushioned and controlled within an economic, social, and political community endowed with enough autonomy to guarantee stability even in a turbulent world environment.

Human-Level Goals

The category of the system-level goals of social evolution subsumes the kind of goals that could ensure a sufficient degree of dynamic stability for national societies to avert the trauma of a violent transformation. Such goals indicate what is functional from the viewpoint of entire nations; how such nations could climb the ladder of evolution by transcending themselves in the process of intersystem convergence. Evolutionary functionality, however, while necessary to avoid violence and breakdown, cannot guarantee humane outcomes. The goals of social evolution need to be further specified. To the category of system-level goals we need to add the further category of goals on the human level.

The achievement of the system-level goals of convergence to a more stable and self-sufficient level of organization is necessary for vulnerable specialist societies, but in itself it is not sufficient to assure desirable conditions. Even transnationally integrated communities could evolve dictatorial, autocratic, and repressive regimes. Such an outcome is always possible but never necessary. A transnational society could also develop democratically. We know that there can be complex systems that allow a high degree of freedom and autonomy for their parts, assuring merely a constant flow of information in the pursuit of shared goals. Such flexible types of coordination dominate in most of the mature ecosystems. Only genetically programmed insect societies and the "hard-wired" control systems made by man operate inflexibly, maintaining order and function at the cost of proscribing the freedom of the subsystems. The human brain itself is a flexibly self-organizing and structure-maintaining system, entirely different from machines and hard-wired computers. Transnational societies could evolve into flexibly coordinated systems on their own convergent organizational level, with optimal autonomy for their human members and for their local and national groups and institutions.

The specification of the human-level goals of social evolution is not a theoretical but a practical task: it must take into account the real values of individuals and their hopes and aspirations. Thus human-level goals cannot be defined in the abstract. At the same time they cannot be defined apart from system-level goals, for whatever their nature, they must prove to be compatible with dynamic stability in society. Without such stability society could not achieve sufficient order and continuity to permit the successful pursuit of any coherent plan of action.

WHAT WE DO MONDAY MORNING: TASKS FOR INDIVIDUALS

We now move another step closer to the solid ground of social reality by descending not only from system-level goals to human-level ones but from general categories to more specific objectives. After all, societies are made up of different people with different talents, skills and aptitudes. Nobody—unless he or she heads and indeed personifies an entire state or nation—can act on behalf of a society as a whole. The goals of social evolution must be broken down into separate tasks that can be realistically tackled by individuals. Scientists, humanists, administrators, and ordinary citizens all have crucial roles to play in steering the next evolution of their society. A few preliminary notes on the tasks indicated for some of the major categories of individuals are given here, not as prescriptions or even as recommendations, but as food for further thought and material for careful reflection.

Tasks for Philosophers and Humanists

Dynamic stability for a society can be achieved in many different ways; the feedbacks and catalytic cycles—the systems of production, consumption and governance—that maintain the social system in its milieu can be functional even if they rob individuals of their basic rights and freedoms. But for individuals the way these cycles operate is of the most immediate concern. Whether the cycles operate through dictatorship and repression or through participation and democracy may be a matter of indifference for society, but it makes all the difference for its members. It is imperative that trade-offs between individual and social rights, between egalitarianism and liberalism, between planning and spontaneity, are carefully weighed. It is likewise imperative that the desirable alternatives are shared and discussed with the general public. Public motivation must be mustered, yet in turbulent periods the public operates under a handicap: changes in societal structures entail a dislocation of the cognitive maps of individuals. Images, beliefs, and routines taken for granted in the past no longer fit; new values, new images, new systems of belief and action, indeed a new morality, are badly needed. To help catalyze such images, values, beliefs, and morality is a task for philosophers, and for humanists in all walks of life. Societal transformation provides an opportunity for selection from among a vast number of alternatives. It places great responsibilities on the shoulders of those who can reflect on the human implications of the alternatives and can propose morally mature guidelines for thinking and action.

Tasks for Social Scientists

People in contemporary societies, especially if they live in highly specialized ones, need detailed and reliable information on the economic, political, social, and ecological ties and relations of their country with the outside world. They need to know under what conditions can specialized vulnerability-inducing relationships be transformed into or replaced by self-reliant generalist capabilities. People in generalist societies, in turn, need to know how the self-reliance of their country can be enhanced and maintained in the face of rapid and frequently unforeseeable change in the international system. A reliable knowledge of the conditions under which society can be sustained and human well-being ensured is needed in all cases. Economists, sociologists, political scientists, even anthropologists and psychologists commanding the required expertise need to become aware of these needs. Their evolutionary task is to place the acquisition of the relevant knowledge on top of their list of research priorities.

Tasks for Natural Scientists and Engineers

Technological advance could decentralize decision making, eliminate dangerous, dirty, and repetitive jobs, and bring people into contact with each other. It could, however, also centralize control and lock people into meaningless, fragmented existences isolated from nature and from each other. The difference is spelled not only by the social, economic, and political structures that make use of the new technologies, but by the technologies themselves. Technologies that automate the everyday activities of people and discourage face-to-face contact lead ultimately to depersonalization and alienation. Technologies that enable distant power centers to spy on people, to control their movements and their self-expressions, prompt applications that stunt personal development and constrain individual freedom. Unmanned factories, automated offices, electronic shopping and communication, remote-controlled agriculture, and the integrated systems of control and management in which they are embedded could automate humankind to the point of removing the sense of meaning, the feel of human contact, and the vital knowledge of importance and responsibility that is essential for healthy personal growth. Indeed, if allowed to evolve unchecked, the new technologies could inject enough information into society to create a plethora of new structures that lock individuals into prearranged niches; society could evolve to the detriment of its human members. But this need not be: new technologies could be created that encourage individual freedom and creativity *and* contact among free and creative individuals. Attention to the effect of new technological innovations, especially in the fields of information, communication, and automation, is a responsibility first of all of those who generate the innovations— the physical scientists and engineers actively engaged in research and development.

Tasks for Administrators

The knowledge required to create a conscious impetus toward systemically functional as well as humanly desirable solutions must be actively promoted and catalyzed. Projects and recommendations must not be left to gather dust on the shelves of libraries or disappear into the bottom files of busy executives. All this calls for funds and organizational ability. Mainstream institutions are not likely to respond to these challenges, embedded as they are in the framework of the national status quo. But individuals in key positions or free agents with the requisite skills could make a crucial difference: they could create and mobilize a critical mass of people, and explore suitable channels of communication with governmental and nongovernmental organizations and with business enterprises. Given today's rapid flow of ideas and instantaneous means of communication, new insights and images could spread rapidly in all strata of the population, and they could gain enough supporters for humanistic causes to give them a chance to take off as potentially influential social movements.

Tasks for Concerned Citizens

The more a society is exposed to rapid and uncontrolled change, the more it is sensitized to new ideas and alternative movements. If there is sufficient diversity in the collective information pool, chances are good that a great variety of causes and movements will surface. The question is, which ones will society select? In 1917 tsarist Russia selected Bolshevism, which, despite its egalitarian ideals and basic humanism, led to greater and greater centralization and to the repressive regime of Stalin. In the 1930s the Weimar Republic selected National Socialism and brought Hitler to power. Even the French Revolution of 1789 gave way to a new elite and a new repression, notwithstanding the noble ideals of Rousseau and Robespierre. Totalitarian solutions are entirely functional from the viewpoint of a social system, even if they repress individual freedom and human rights. Failure to do one's best to counter such solutions is an act of moral irresponsibility. The existence of evolutionary laws in history is not an excuse for passivity: the laws allow multiple outcomes and permit concerned people to influence the course of events in favor of consciously selected solutions.

Purposive and effective action in a period of societal transformation can create and promote ideas and movements that can grow into new foundations for people and societies. In the language of evolutionary biology, scientists, humanists, administrators, and concerned citizens who accept the challenge of defining evolutionary goals and acting on them constitute the societal subspecies which, coming from the periphery, invade the destabilized centers of power and replace the previously dominant—and now moribund—societal species. In the still more applicable language of dynamic systems theory, the goals injected by purposive actors into the turbulent dynamics of a bifurcation are the stable attractors that capture the states of the destabilized social system within a new and humanistic dynamic regime.

It is altogether possible, as Jonas Salk points out in *The Anatomy of Reality,* that the ability to look ahead, to imagine, to reason, to think, to weigh, and to judge exists strongly enough in the minds of a sufficient number of individuals that a critical mass may exist which can influence humankind to respond more appropriately than we do today to the challenges of evolution. If a critical mass of concerned people would accept the challenge of purposive intervention in contemporary social evolution, the future of humanity could yet be assured. Human societies would no longer evolve haphazardly, for better or for worse. People would govern the course of bifurcations and help create societies consistent both with the evolutionary imperatives of system stability and with their own values and aspirations.

The evolution of our societies, and therewith the future of our species, is now in our hands. If we make use of our capacity to think rationally and act purposefully, we can defuse immediate threats and promote the creation of more mature, more autonomous, more dynamically stable societies. Only by becoming conscious of evolution can we make evolution conscious, and only by conscious evolution can we have any assurance that we can survive the awesome combination of highly evolved order and complexity in our brains and as yet immature and underdeveloped order in our societies.

9

An Analytical Postscript: Case Studies of Social Bifurcations

Bifurcations are critical junctures in the evolution of human societies—as they are in the evolution of all systems in the third state. They are especially critical in contemporary societies, since the costs of undesirable outcomes could be disastrous. Assuming that the choice among alternative outcomes need not be left to chance, conscious action at points of social bifurcation needs to be thoroughly effective. This means action that is purposive and well informed. The principal objectives of such action have been outlined above: they consist of the system-level goals of creating sustainable, dynamically stable societies, and within the wide range of possibilities provided by this requirement to achieve human-level goals of justice and humanism. The aim of the case studies of this analytical postscript is complementary: it is to help specify concrete strategies for the achievement of these goals by noting how some major bifurcations occurred in the past, and assessing how they are likely to take place in the future.

The studies analyze historical and prospective social bifurcations in reference to the three principal types suggested in Chapter 5: bifurcations due to the destabilizing effect of technological innovations ('T-bifurcations'), bifurcations due to instabilities induced by conflicts and conquests ('C-bifurcations'), and bifurcations triggered by the internal collapse of the dominant institutions owing to mushrooming economic and social crises ('E-bifurcations').

T-BIFURCATIONS

The relentless spread of modern technologies creates imbalances within contemporary societies. Established values are uprooted, new expectations are encouraged, and, as they are frequently unfulfilled, frustration and discontent are fueled. Technologies spreading from a handful of industrialized and postindustrialized countries to the far corners of the world change people's lives. They trigger social change, but at high human cost.

The analyses that follow aim to shed light on the depth and the nature of the social and institutional changes needed to cope with major technological innovations. The first, brief study refers to the past: it shows that our technologies may be new but the kind of societal impact they have is not: technological innovations were responsible for some major and unexpected social transformations already in classical antiquity. The second, more detailed study concerns the present: it outlines the formidable challenges posed by the technological innovations of what is justly called the second industrial revolution.

The Hoplite Revolution

Technological innovations have triggered social transformations in the past; only the dimensions of the challenges posed by current technologies are new and not the challenges themselves. Humankind's first experiment with democracy is a case in point. Known as the hoplite revolution, it was a successful response to the challenge of a little-known—but highly significant—technological innovation.

The innovation concerned warfare. Around 700 B.C., iron became common and inexpensive enough for average citizens to possess. It was used to make offensive weapons as well as protective armor. This seemingly minor innovation was enough to effect some truly basic changes in Hellenic societies. In the Mycenaean age, warfare was the privileged domain of aristocrats, who could afford to purchase horses and bronze armor; chariots and cavalry played the dominant role. The privileged few led the battles and reaped the rewards of victory. But when iron technologies became widely available, military prowess came to the foot soldier. Against an infantry clad in armor and wielding iron thrusting spears cavalry was almost always defeated. The "hoplite phalanx," as it was called (*hoplite* comes from the Greek *hoplon,* meaning "tool"), relied on compactness rather than on individual action as it broke through the enemy ranks to throw their line into chaos.

Hoplites became the most effective fighters in the Mediterranean world. Within fifty years they eroded the power of the aristocrats and took over the business of governance as well as that of warfare. Hoplites were not whipped into battle, as Herodotus writes that the Persians were. They fought on the basis of consensus developed through the logic of argument. Consequently the power that came to the citizens through the spread of iron technology triggered a reorganization that, in the Hellenic society of the epoch, was expressed in the principle of *isonomia*—equal participation in government. The social transformation that was thus created laid the foundations of Western democracy: the advent of the hoplites is aptly called a revolution.

The Second Industrial Revolution

Unlike the revolution of the hoplites, the revolution triggered by the new technologies of information, communication, and automation is not history: it is living reality. We cannot as yet foresee its outcome but can already assess its nature and dimensions.

Probably more than 90 percent of all the scientific research and development ever undertaken in history has occurred in the period since the beginning of World War II. Scientific R&D, which has accelerated continuously in most countries, gave societies the power of the atom as well as the power of information, communication, and automation. It has put unprecedented power in the hands of those who control the new technologies and now threatens the lives of those who are exposed to their unreflective use—or their purposive misuse. Nuclear technologies, for example, can be used in explosives, and they can destroy the human population of the planet twenty times over. They can also render the biosphere unfit for life higher than insects and grass. But if nuclear technologies are used for peaceful purposes, deserts can be irrigated, fresh water can be made universally available, machinery basic for industry and agriculture can be powered, and life and prosperity can be assured not only for six but for ten or more billion people. The planet's carrying capacity can be enlarged and the demands of an increasingly large and increasingly prosperous population can be satisfied.

However, such a "nuclear paradise" would call for a major reorganization of contemporary societies. It is doubtful whether people today have the vision and the will to carry it out. Einstein may have been right when he said that the unleashed power of the atom has changed everything save our modes of thinking. If in the nuclear age humanity is to prosper—and even if it is merely to survive—current modes of thinking and behavior would have to change radically. Our most basic forms of social, economic, and political organization will have to be reformed. It is by no means clear whether the twentieth-century system of nation-states could survive into the twenty-first century: the system may be too prone to conflict and too adverse to cooperation to permit the spread of nuclear technologies for peaceful uses alone. It is also questionable whether the current economic and financial system could survive—its concentration of economic power in the hands of national governments and giant transnational corporations may be inimical to the development and application of the technologies needed not only to support the wealthy and the educated, but also to feed, house, employ, and educate the poor and the illiterate.

The problems are not eliminated if, instead of mainly nuclear, a mix of new energy technologies is used. Indeed, a proper mix of renewable and nonrenewable, nuclear and solar-based technologies may prove to be the optimum solution to the energy problems of our economies; but a mix of energy sources would require further societal adjustments. Solar technologies harness the energy of the sun, and, as such energy reaches the earth in a diffuse form, the applications of the technologies tend to be decentralized and small-scale. To use solar power as a main energy source for metroindustrial complexes would call for covering large surface areas with solar cells, solar towers, windmills, or other technological devices. Since this is both impracticable and environmentally hazardous, solar technologies would best be used in small, decentralized economic units. Thus attention would have to shift to many as yet underdeveloped rural areas. Farmers and villagers would have to be given the opportunity to develop the technologies in light of their own needs and preferences. This would call for major shifts in the allocation of priorities between capitals and hinterlands, shifts that many governments advocate in principle but few are willing to carry out in practice.

Mastering the information technologies of the second industrial revolution calls for similarly profound societal changes. The gap between advanced information societies and the majority of developing countries in the Third World is growing with astonishing speed. It polarizes the international economic system. Multinationals are not likely to be effective in bridging the gap, as their business is business and not the service of socioeconomic equality and justice. If current trends are not turned around, massive worldwide unemployment would result as automated control technologies—the already famed "robotics"—replace unskilled and semiskilled human labor in country after country and field after field. Japan expects to have unmanned factories by the turn of the century, and U.S. companies predict the advent of paperless, fully computerized offices. National economies relying on the comparative cheapness of manual or semiskilled labor would find that their comparative advantages have evaporated.

The latest information technologies also deplace jobs in the advanced information sector. Unlike previous information technologies that permitted people to do things they earlier could *not* do, the new technologies also do things that people rely on being *able* to do. Modern computers reduce the number of draftsmen and engineers required to see projects through to completion. They reduce the number of clerks and secretaries needed in business and administration. They even deplace a number of professionals, such as lawyers and medical doctors. Computerized "expert systems" diagnose illnesses, identify errors, give financial and legal advice, prepare taxes, and do an increasing number of jobs hitherto entrusted to people. Indeed, employment in the information sector of advanced societies has all but stopped growing in recent years, and may actually begin to shrink.

The technologies of the second industrial revolution are truly revolutionary. Not only are they major advances over previous technologies, but they also require major transformations in the societies that make use of them. A postindustrial society based on abundant and dense energy sources and on information, robotics, and automation reaches new heights in autonomy: it progressively detaches itself from geographic constraints. It generates its own energies and produces its own raw materials with less and less dependence on the endowments of its milieu. This could lead to a brusque rupture of geocultural ties which evolved over centuries; customs, forms of organization, and systems of beliefs mediating between society and environment could suddenly become irrelevant or actually obstructive. The traditional aptitudes of the work force, strongly tied to social, cultural, and historical customs and traditions, could become all but useless. Skills essential in a preindustrial community may be marginally useful in an industrial society, and could prove to be entirely superfluous in a postindustrial one.

The new technologies make distinctions between city and countryside almost as irrelevant as geographic location. Space and time constraints are all but eliminated by telecommunications and high-speed transportation. There is no further need for urban megacomplexes; high-tech producers and consumers can just as well live in decentralized suburban or rural settings.

The new technologies are not passive "menus" from which individuals, firms, and societies can pick and choose according to their capacities and appetites. The technologies come in mutually supporting clusters, engulfing the user in a vast array of procedures that he or she may be hard put to master and manage. For example, CIM—computer-integrated manufacturing—is a rational innovation for a wide variety of manufacturers. It integrates the entire manufacturing process from the original product concept to the procurement of components, their assembly and inventory management, and their transport and marketing. CIM calls for CAD (computer-aided design) and for OA (office automation). Economic logic, and the survival imperative of firms in high-pressure competition, dictates that these clusters of technologies be used together. Success seems to crown the efforts of those who master the full range of the available technologies and do not hesitate to innovate wherever and whenever innovation promises benefits.

But in the late twentieth century, success of this kind may be a short-term affair and its pursuit a double-edged sword. The innovators may find that in creating a postindustrial enterprise in an industrial (not to mention a preindustrial) society, they have bit off more than they could chew. Or they may succeed in mastering their own procedures, only to find that they are overproducing goods that are in limited demand. Traditional production systems geared to supply standardized mass-produced goods are not easy to transform into footloose, decentralized, and personalized goods-producing enterprises—especially if the transformation requires firing much of the work force. Consumers in today's societies may become impoverished and alienated by depersonalized robots, even if the robots churn out personalized goods and custom-tailored services. Mistrust combined with lack of buying power could thwart the shining rationality of managers keen on technological innovations.

The technologies of the second industrial revolution are not simple extensions of the classical industrial technologies with improvements in quality and quantity, speed and reliability. The new technologies are fundamentally different, and they call for fundamentally new mind-sets in individuals and new forms of social and economic (and hence also political) organization in society.

The new technologies are clearly aligned with long-term trends in the evolution of human societies: they conduce to high levels of autonomy and greater complexity, and access to abundant, and in part also highly dense, energy sources. But to achieve the bifurcation that still separates us from fully evolved postindustrial societies, we would need to transform our thinking as well as our social structures. Ignoring "soft" sociocultural factors would soon turn them into surprisingly hard and obstructive realities.

C-BIFURCATIONS

History provides a rich terrain for the exploration of conflict-induced bifurcations in the development of societies. Unlike technological and economic bifurcations, these dramatic—and often also traumatic—events are normally perceived as revolutions in the traditional sense of the term.

C-bifurcations (the classical variety of revolutions) do not necessarily mean a complete break with the past; historians have often pointed to elements of continuity. In the case of the French Revolution of 1789, Tocqueville found that it accomplished many goals pursued by French kings since Louis XI, and Lord Acton announced that it brought the political structure of French society into line with long-established traditions in its social structure. But historians have also discovered that revolutions change the established institutions of society, adapting them to the forces and factors—technological, economic, or political—that brought down the previous regime. Taking an optimistic evolutionary view, Henri Sée sought to demonstrate that revolutions speed up rates of growth, purge ossified institutions, and establish spiritual goals that stimulate further development. Later historians, such as Chalmers Johnson, offered detailed analyses of modern revolutions conceived as the adjustment of the state apparatus to societal dysfunctions. Although there is still no agreement among contemporary historians as to what causes revolutions, whether they follow a uniform pattern and what their consequences are, most scholars would now agree that revolutions, despite certain continuities, also produce discontinuities that are rapid and significant. Many would also claim that the changes can be understood as reorientations of society to radically altered conditions. Revolutions seem to be functional from the viewpoint of creating institutions, behaviors, and values that respond to the threats and challenges that destabilized the "ancient regime."

The world wars of the twentieth century produced the widest variety of conflict-triggered revolutions in recent history. Among them, two stand out in virtue of their worldwide impact: the transformation of tsarist Russia into the Soviet Union and the transformation of the Weimar Republic into the Third Reich.[1]

Bifurcation in Tsarist Russia

The rise of the Communist regime in Russia, like that of the Nazi regime in Germany, was triggered by the giant wave of political, social, and economic instability created by World War I. This was a "total" war for Europe: millions of casualties were suffered; immense debts were accumulated; social relationships were drastically altered; and economic, financial, and basic moral resources were used up. By the end the experience had exhausted almost all combatants, and states lacking the resilience to cope were driven to the point of breakdown.

Although the revolutionary changes that took place in Russia in 1917 and in Germany fifteen years later were triggered by the instabilities created by World War I, they had deep historical roots. Russia's failure to modernize its social, economic, and political structures during the nineteenth century left it unstable and rigid; it was readily destabilized by a major war. Indeed, failure in the 1904 war with Japan had already led to a nearly successful revolt in 1905. Attempts within Russia to accelerate reforms, such as those of Stolypin, were frustrated by conservative political forces. But economic growth, industrialization, and social unrest proceeded apace and created growing tensions. The result was a government that alienated its middle-class supporters while driving the peasants and workers toward ever more violent acts that antagonized the foes of the regime. By 1914 the nation was so divided internally that the outbreak of war merely delayed the revolution by momentarily redirecting crucial social and political energies.

Nicholas II's inability to govern created a deep crisis as the Russian armies suffered a series of humiliating defeats. The tsar's decision to take personal command only led to his being personally blamed for the failures. Corruption, aggravated by the ascension of Rasputin over the tsarina—because of his strange power to control the hemophilia of the crown prince—meant that the state bureaucracy was even less able to supply desperately needed arms, clothing, and food. By February 1917, food riots had broken out, the Russian economic and political system had collapsed, and the Romanov dynasty had been toppled.

The speed and thoroughness of the collapse of the tsarist regime surprised even Sukhanov and others who had devoted their lives to the revolutionary overthrow of the government. Even more surprising was the final outcome of the revolution. Stalin and the Petrograd leadership had supported the provisional government for months. *Pravda* actually printed articles opposing plans by Lenin and Trotsky to "telescope" stages by seizing power in November. At the critical moment Lenin himself despaired of success, and only Trotsky was able to dissuade him from fleeing to Finland. But the situation at home became unsustainable and ripe for change. The war had precipitated the collapse of the tsarist regime, and Allied demands that Russia honor its treaties and continue fighting made it impossible for the provisional government to solve the basic problems that had caused the February revolution. The Bolsheviks succeeded in stepping in at the crucial moment. Even though they were but a relatively minor political movement—a "peripheral isolate"—they could seize power in the power vacuum and chaos of the day. Divided among themselves and scattered from Geneva to Brooklyn, their ideas were often contradictory and their strategies unclear. But Lenin came out with his "April Theses," and his ideas and strategy became increasingly attractive in the deepening crisis. His slogan "Bread, Land, and Peace," promised to meet the most basic needs of the masses. It levered the Bolsheviks into position as leaders of the urban workers, whose prewar violence had been contained only briefly by patriotic appeals. Internal class antagonisms were greatly exacerbated by oppressive policies, poor military performance, and gross corruption. Increasing radicalism among urban groups as well as among peasants and soldiers, combined with Lenin's political and oratorical skills, Trotsky's genius for military organization, and the efficiency of the revitalized Bolshevik apparatus tipped the scales by November: the Bolsheviks seized the reigns of power.

Bifurcation in the Weimar Republic

Germany's transformation from the Weimar Republic to the Third Reich was less telescoped in time than the events in Russia but was hardly less dramatic. Having entered World War I as the strongest power on the Continent, Germany's defeat created a major social trauma among its people. Scapegoats had to be found to explain how a magnificent army, countless acts of personal courage, and extensive national sacrifices culminated in humiliating losses of territory, sovereignty, foreign colonies, a powerful fleet, and great industrial might. Mutual recriminations between conservatives and socialists, republicans and monarchists, and between various segments of society and Jews led to serious internal fragmentation. The rapid introduction of modern technology into Wilhelmian Germany had already destabilized the traditional institutions and created deep and widespread alienation. Compounded by defeat and the humiliation of the Treaty of Versailles, social institutions collapsed and revolts became a frequent occurrence. Street fighting was rampant, "political" murders like those of Erzberger and Rathenau became common, and civil war seemed imminent.

War debts, the penury inflicted by the Treaty of Versailles, foreign interventions, and a devastating inflation kept the German economy in crisis until the Young Plan was instituted in 1932. By then the Depression (precipitated by the failure of an Austrian bank, which broke the essential cycle of payments) had driven unemployment to all-time highs. The divided Reichstag was unable to maintain a majority; after 1930, government was by presidential decree. Yet the president, Field Marshal Hindenburg, was too aged and fragile to exercise the needed leadership. He was easily manipulated by intriguing army officers like Schleicher and Papen.

The competition between these two officers was a major factor in Hitler's rise to power in January 1933. In times of relative normalcy, Adolf Hitler, the Austrian corporal who had failed as an architect and whose accent was so alien that Prussians ridiculed it, would have been an unlikely choice in a society as sophisticated as the Weimar Republic. His party platform was so contradictory that he himself promised not to implement it, and his previous attempts to seize power (during the 1923 financial crisis) had ended in imprisonment. Yet, in the chaos of a destabilized society, Hitler was able to mobilize political support. A month after announcing that there was "not the slightest chance" of the Nazis coming to power, and three days after asserting that Hitler could never take over the government, Hindenburg himself named Hitler chancellor. Papen had persuaded Hindenburg to "tame" Hitler by giving him responsibilities and letting him demonstrate his incompetence. But Hitler was by this time the head of the largest party in the Reichstag, and his coalition gave him a real though slight majority. His personal appeal to the masses gave the disintegrating society a sense of unity. In the wake of the Reichstag fire—whose cause remains obscure to this day—he used the power of party and of propaganda to build up his charisma and make himself invincible.

Hitler's policies were not without appeal to the remaining wealthy classes since he promised to respect property, prevent strikes, and fight communism. His appeal for the masses was reinforced by aligning himself with an anti-Semitic tradition that traced its roots to the Middle Ages. Extolling the virtues of the Aryan race and the destiny of the German state, and promising to revenge lost wealth and prestige by bringing Germany to the pinnacle of world power, Hitler's atavistic policies and personality had the crucial effect: it overcame the frustration and alienation of the postwar decade and rallied society to a new cause—however inhuman and violent that cause may appear in historical perspective.

The rise of the Bolsheviks in Russia and the rise of Hitler in Germany are dissimilar in many particulars; no attempt is made here to draw moral and ideological parallels. Yet, like more recent revolutionary transformations in China, Cuba, Iran, Chile, Nicaragua, Iraq, Libya, and hosts of other Third World countries, they exhibit the basic dynamic of conflict-triggered C-bifurcations.

E-BIFURCATIONS

Bifurcations triggered by economic and social crises are of particular relevance to the future: they may become comparatively widespread in coming years. While such E-bifurcations occurred sporadically in history, a massive wave of economic-instability-induced societal changes may come about in the last decade of this century because of a fateful combination of population growth and resource deprivation. The problems created by these factors are further exacerbated by the increasingly unbearable burden placed on today's economies by military expenditures.

The spread of modern technologies plays havoc with the demographic balance of traditional societies. New health-care technologies and improved diets decrease infant mortality and extend life expectancy in country after country. But they do not directly impact on traditional desires for large families: the demographic curve shows a significant delay in the decrease of the birthrate.

Many societies in the developing world find themselves unable to keep up with the demands of their people. Under the weight of a rapidly growing human population, with exponentially increasing demands, the supply of several kinds of basic resources will inevitably run low. Such resource squeezes could provoke severe economic recession and accompanying social and political instabilities. While the threshold of resource-deprivation-based instability is likely to vary from society to society, depending on the specific nature of their systems of production and consumption and on the level of efficiency and discipline of the people, it seems clear that beyond certain limits all social structures will become critically unstable.

Looking at the resource picture on the level of the globe as a whole, there is cause for concern. World population has grown explosively during the twentieth century and will continue to grow rapidly in coming decades. Even a reduction in fertility rates cannot significantly slow the still ongoing explosion of the world population: some 35 percent of the world's present population are children under fifteen years of age. Even if those who now enter the age of fertility have fewer children than their parents, the number of people who will be *added* to the human population in the last quarter of this century would still be greater than the entire world population at the beginning of this century (2.05 billion people, compared to 1.6 billion). The over six billion humans who will populate this earth by the year 2000 will also demand far more resources per capita than any generation has ever demanded before. It seems likely that humanity will consume more resources during the second half of the twentieth century than it did during the previous three hundred centuries of its existence as a dominant species.

The fact that most of the increase in the world population takes place in the poor developing regions of the world does not improve the picture. Tradition-bound poor countries would have to develop new and optimally efficient technologies to access, store, and utilize a wide variety of energy and material resources. This would be entirely feasible in principle, but it does call for a major reorganization of the dominant systems of production, consumption, and governance.

For the most part contemporary societies would have to join together in more embracing social and economic communities to ensure a broader resource and technology base. As discussed in Chapter 8, a shift to a transnational level of organization is needed to bring together small or insufficiently developed or poorly endowed societies in sufficiently autonomous regional structures. Within the narrower confines of nation-states the combination of expanding population and shrinking resource availability causes deepening crises. Governments attempt to cope with them through a series of emergency measures; national governance often transforms into crisis-management. Not surprisingly, such efforts do not produce lasting results. Where a basic restructuring of society is called for, patchwork solutions are at best temporary palliatives; mostly they create deeper problems.

The logistical curve of increasing resource demand cannot be sustained indefinitely. The supply curve is already dipping below the demand curve. If we disaggregate the global picture by major resource categories, we see the roots of the major factors of instability.

The Energy Instability

Modern societies are highly energy-intensive. This is not surprising: as already noted, energy use is positively correlated with level of historical development. Today's world still runs primarily on fossil fuels although these fuels—oil, coal and natural gas—cannot remain for long the staple energy source of a globally extended technological civilization. The U.S. Geological Survey estimates that the known reserves of readily extractable oil would be enough to last humanity roughly sixty years at current rates of consumption. Most of these reserves are concentrated in the Persian Gulf; major new discoveries elsewhere appear more and more unlikely. The North Sea may go into decline before the end of the century, and the North Slope in Alaska is likely to do so as well. Mexico and other Third World oil producers outside the Persian Gulf will soon need their entire production for domestic use. Some experts estimate that by about the turn of the century, it will take more energy to explore for new oil in the United States than the wells are likely to produce.

Given the collapse of world oil prices in the mid-1980s, global production is likely to remain high. It would then begin a steep decline by the 1990s. A rapid depletion of global reserves could have several untoward consequences. A precious raw material for the chemical and pharmaceutical industries could be made unavailable before substitutes are developed. Economically competitive alternative energy sources may not be developed in time—especially if oil prices remain low. And the carbon dioxide content of the atmosphere could be rapidly increased with the probability of a significant and virtually irreversible heating up of the earth's surface—and major changes in the world's climate.

Alternative energies would have to be developed rapidly and efficiently. The current state of R&D in this area is unsatisfactory. The technologies of producing energy from heavy crude, tar sands, and shale are energy- and water-intensive; they are also expensive and have a heavy impact on the environment. The use of coal encounters many problems in large-scale use, including acid drainage, the denuding of lands in strip mining, and subsidence and black-lung disease in pit mining. Natural gas may exist in large quantities, but many of the major reserves are in remote areas, such as the polar icecap, where exploitation is both expensive and damaging to the environment.

As already noted, solar and other renewable energies are safe but highly diffuse: big cities and major industrial centers could make only marginal use of them. Much R&D would be required to bring down the cost of solar technologies and make them available for all the decentralized uses where they could replace fossil and nuclear technologies. Dung and firewood are products of nature, but if they are burned in large quantities, forests are cut down, lands are denuded, and nature becomes inhospitable and unproductive.

It might appear that nuclear technologies have pride of place among humanity's long-term energy alternatives. Yet here, too, great investment of time and talent is required to make the technology appropriate for worldwide use. The near-catastrophe at Three Mile Island in the United States, and the meltdown at Chernobyl in the Soviet Union have been dramatic demonstrations of fission-reactor vulnerability and the threat this poses to populations even in distant lands. Fission reactors are difficult to make accident-proof and impossible to render attack-proof. Given the increasingly sophisticated weapons available to terrorists, police cordons around reactor sites are insufficient; attackers may fire lightweight rockets from any rooftop or backyard in an area large enough to preclude effective surveillance. The risks in the gamble on nuclear fission will increase proportionately to the extent that the world becomes more tense and polarized and the technology of its weapons is further perfected.

Nuclear *fusion* technologies could become available in coming decades and could produce relatively safe and low-cost electrical energy. But the development of nuclear fusion, like that of any alternative energy technology, calls for a major shift in social priorities and a new economic upswing with a significant level of equity among national economies. As of the mid-1980s neither the capital nor the infrastructure is given in any but a small handful of the world's nations to develop, build and operate fusion reactors.

The problem with energy is not that humanity could not produce enough of it, but that to produce enough at acceptable cost, at acceptable risk, and in a form fitted to end uses, major changes would have to be made in today's production and consumption structures. In the absence of such changes, the world energy situation will sooner or later turn seriously destabilizing for the majority of contemporary societies.

The Food Instability

The problem of meeting demand with supply in the area of staple foods is even more serious. If six or eight billion people are to survive on this earth and raise families, access to staple foods must increase significantly, especially in the poorest and least developed societies.

The production of food, unlike the production of renewable energies, faces definite physical limits: the amount of prime agricultural land on earth is limited. Of the planet's land surface, the area not covered with ice is roughly 134 million square kilometers. World agriculture is limited to about 18 million square kilometers, roughly 13.4 percent of the above total. But even this surface is subject to diminution: an estimated 150 thousand square kilometers of productive land is lost each year to urban sprawl, soil erosion, pollution, and the advance of deserts. Productivity can be considerably but not indefinitely increased on the remaining surfaces—the food-producing capacity of the earth's ecosystems have certain, even if generous, upper limits.

Food shortages at the present time are due above all to the

mismanagement of existing lands and the failure to increase long-term productivity. Mechanized agriculture is nonsustainable because of its fossil-fuel-based energy intensity and the chemical overexploitation of the soils; traditional agriculture in turn is nonsustainable because of its wasteful underproductivity and the overcropping and overgrazing that are its likely result.

Current policies and practices create a nonsustainable situation in country after country. While as recently as 1950 most of the developing countries were self-sufficient in the production of staple foods, today hardly any of them can do without major food imports. Total Third World cereal imports have risen from 14 million tons in midcentury to over 100 million tons in the 1980s, and may reach 200 million tons by the year 2000. Self-sufficiency ratios dip correspondingly, from near 100 percent to the lower 70 percent range. The areas of shortfall include cereals as well as livestock and dairy products.

Marine resources, while essential for ecological balance in the biosphere, currently provide only a limited amount of food: total fishery harvests are stagnant at about 70 million metric tons per year. The exploitation of additional species (such as squid and krill) and integrated management systems covering vast ocean areas could increase the share of marine foods in the diet of the world population. But efficient mariculture, the same as efficient, energy- and sustainability-conscious agriculture, calls for major investment, high-level R&D, expert application of the technologies, and a broad basis in international cooperation. The rich countries would have to take the initiative, for the poor countries can hardly be expected to muster all these factors. And production alone is not enough: attention would have to focus on distribution as well. In many countries even if food production rose to adequate per-capita levels, large segments of the population would still be left without adequate supplies.

Water, Forest, and Genetic Resource Instabilities

Similar problems appear on the horizon also with respect to other biospheric resources, including water and forests. Water for drinking, sanitary uses, industrial purposes, and irrigation is already in short supply, especially in Africa and South Asia. Yet demand for water will increase as supplies per capita decrease, creating major shortages in the poorest and most populated regions. The cost of water is likely to rise in the 1990s, causing problems for all countries, including the industrialized economies, whose demand will increase with the introduction of such water-intensive technologies as the production of synthetic fuels from coal and shale.

The disappearance of the world's major tropical rainforests compounds the problem of natural resources. The area of forests in the developing countries has declined by half during the twentieth century. Tropical watersheds are threatened by overgrazing and soil erosion, causing floods, disrupting downstream irrigation systems, and diminishing the size of crops.

The disappearance of forests has repercussions in the area of ecological diversity. Genetic diversity is a necessity rather than a luxury; while the full effect of major losses in genetic materials is not entirely known, it is likely to seriously impair the viability of human habitats as well as cut into world food production. The flattening of diversity is due in part to the disappearance of tropical forests harboring some 40 percent of living species, and in part to the shortsighted practice of modern agriculture to plant only a few varieties of high-yield crops.

The fact that technologies exist for conserving and recycling almost all basic resources does not guarantee that supply will effectively match demand: as the historical examples cited in Chapter 5 illustrate, the mere availability of a technology is not a guarantee of its effective application. In today's world, inappropriate technologies fail to penetrate the operative structures of traditional societies—there are many "cathedrals in the desert," costly dams, highways, steel mills, and other structures that stand misused and ultimately unused, monuments to inflated leadership egos and naive technological optimism.

The Employment Instability

Employment is among the most basic factors of instability in contemporary societies. A large proportion of today's global work force is unemployed, perhaps as many as 600 million. The number of those who are underemployed or occupy jobs ill fitted to their qualifications and capacities is certain to be much higher still.

The imbalance in the industrial division of labor between advanced and underdeveloped countries is at the root of the global employment problem. The work force grows in countries and regions that are industrially backward and have relatively few jobs to offer in consequence. Over 630 million people are expected to swell the potential work force of developing countries by the year 2000, whereas the addition to the work force of the industrialized countries may be no more than about 20 million.

Practically all the "factors of production"—capital, access to energy and raw materials, evolved infrastructures, technologies, and skills—are concentrated in the advanced industrial economies. Only manpower and some natural resources are available in greater abundance in the poor parts of the world. But the value of natural resources depends on whether or not synthetic substitutes are found for them, and the value of manpower is relative to the needs of modern industry. Multinational corporations, the biggest employers of the developing countries' surplus labor, show a definite preference for automated production systems. Automated systems ensure high profits and a growing share of the market; in the long run they are cheaper than people. Also, they do not demand higher wages or go on strike. Machines are replacing people not only in the high-tech fields, but also in branches of industry that were hitherto the preserve of less developed countries, such as textiles, shoes, clothing, simple manufacturing, automobile and appliance assembly, and electronic components production. By the end of the century the work force engaged to produce necessary goods and perform necessary services may well be but a fraction of what it is today.

Champions of the new technologies claim that fears of "structural unemployment" are groundless; that the experience of the first industrial revolution will be repeated with new jobs created in sufficient numbers to replace those that were lost. But the first industrial revolution took almost a century to bring its benefits to the masses, and with today's rapid population increase developing countries may have no more than a decade to achieve this feat. It is difficult to see how they could achieve it, lacking the necessary capital, even the facilities for education and skill training.

For the time being the new technologies replace only about 20 percent of the jobs they eliminate. They create unemployment even in the industrialized regions: the secretariat of the Organization for Economic Cooperation and Development (OECD) estimates that unemployment in the advanced member countries in North America, Western Europe, and Japan is of the order of 40 million persons—a conservative figure which, according to some experts, should be increased by as much as 40 percent to correspond to reality. Clearly, the impact of the new technologies in the less developed world is considerably greater. If not given adequate opportunities for work, the hundreds of millions who will enter the work force between now and the end of the century in Asia, Africa, and Latin America will be major factors of social and political instability. The fact is that already today some one billion people in Asia, Africa, and Latin America live from hand to mouth, on the bare edge of subsistence.

Financial Instabilities

Economic statistics show that the gap between economically advanced and the underdeveloped countries continues to widen. At the beginning of the 1980s, GNP per capita was close to $10,000 in the industrialized free-market economies, while it averaged under $250 in the least developed countries. Economists project that the figure will rise to over $11,000 by the end of the century in the industrialized North, while it will reach no more than $311 in the poor countries of the South. Of course, such global statistics mask local differences in the distribution of wealth and also fail to take into account differences in the buying power of the dollar, the unit of measurement. However, they do give a rough indication of the dimensions and the continued growth of the financial gap between the rich and the poor of this world.

The international economic and financial system seems unable to cope with the gaps and inequities of the distribution of wealth. As advanced countries protect their markets from competing imports from the Third World, the restricted access of poor countries to major world markets creates a chronic shortage of hard currency. Because of rising costs at home and decreasing incomes from abroad, Third World countries chalk up growing current account deficits. They are forced to borrow from the governments and private banks of industrialized countries and from multilateral financial institutions such as the International Monetary Fund and

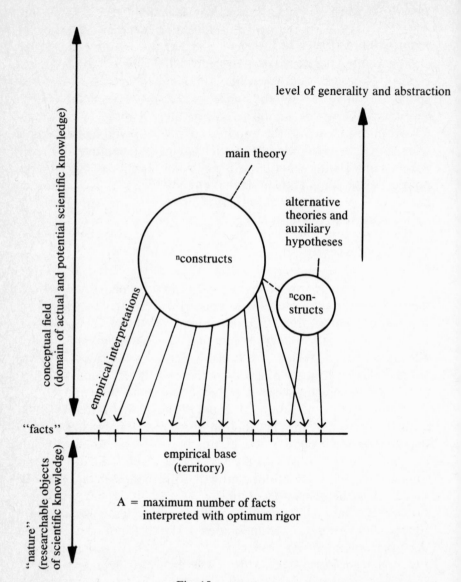

Fig. 15

the World Bank. The international financial system created after
World War II at Bretton Woods was never intended to handle the
amount of "sovereign borrowing" now taking place. Its responses
to the international debt crisis are slow and frequently inadequate.
When a sovereign country cannot meet its repayment schedule,
the debt is rolled over or new loan packages are put together to bail
out the ailing economy. Such solutions are temporary palliatives;
in the long run they merely increase the amount of the accumulated
debt, which, in 1986, reached one trillion dollars. Under prevailing
economic, social, and political conditions the chances of its repayment are slight. Rollovers and rescue packages postpone the day of
reckoning but cannot do away with it.

The situation is more serious than is generally recognized. The
indebted poor countries in the South are actually transferring
money to their rich cousins in the North: they pay more on
outstanding debts and interests than they receive in aid and investment flows. Already in 1983, these "reverse transfers" of capital
came to an estimated $21 billion.

A tidal wave of debt repudiations could cause a major crisis in
the international financial system with repercussions on the national finances of creditor countries as well. Well over half of the
outstanding loans to developing countries have been issued by the
major commercial banks of a few industrialized economies, primarily the United States. If Argentina, Brazil, and Mexico, for
example, were to repudiate their debts and stop payments on
principal and interest, almost 30 percent of the private capital of
the nine largest U.S. banks would be jeopardized. These banks,
unlike sovereign states, are liable to go bankrupt unless bailed out
by their governments. Whether they go under or are saved by
massive infusions of capital, the domestic and international consequences are likely to be considerable.

Some success in the country-by-country renegotiation of over-
due debts should not blind us to the fact that the shortsightedness
of both creditor and debtor countries created a time bomb that is
still ticking.

No review of the economic and social problems of contemporary
nation-states would be complete without mention of the financial
impact of the arms race. The world's governments together spend
close to $1,000 billion per year on military establishments. This is

twice as much as the amount spent on growing food, five times that devoted to housing, and 2,300 times the cost of internationally supervised peacekeeping. It is equivalent to the annual income of 2.5 billion people in the underdeveloped world. Overmilitarization in a world of growing economic disparities, social unrest, and political volatility is a risky condition. In a world where pound for pound there are more bombs than food, security is dubious and overspending is certain. In such a world, a great variety of C- and E-bifurcations are just around the corner.

The above studies highlight some of the sources of instability in contemporary nation-states. There are others, for technological impacts, consequences of conflicts, and the effects of growing disparities between demand and supply exist in many forms and areas. But the purpose of this analytical postscript is not to catalogue such problems but to assist purposive action by illuminating the nature of the instability-induced bifurcations faced by many, if not all, contemporary societies.

Although the problems are serious, there is no cause for despair. The bifurcations of contemporary societies can be steered. Doing so takes more than the exercise of military force, and the use of traditional and now superannuated principles of governance. Instead, it takes the best insights we can muster into the dynamics of evolution in nature and in society. When joined with a thorough familiarity with the specifics of each situation, the principles of a grand evolutionary synthesis can inform actions capable of ensuring life and well-being in a world on the threshold of a new millennium—and a new age.

From the Midnight Notebook

This is an exciting age, perhaps the most exciting in the history of humanity. We live at the precise moment when we are simultaneously becoming aware of the processes that evolve our societies and acquiring mastery of the technologies that determine *how* they evolve. We live at the conjunction of knowledge and power. Whether we also live at the moment of emerging wisdom remains to be seen.

Once again, we are not strangers in an alien, mechanistic universe. The grand synthesis of evolution reintegrates us with nature. Our distant ancestors considered themselves an organic part of all that exists, expressing their belief through myth and confirming it through magic. Our not-so-distant forebears thought they knew better and put man above nature, and indeed beyond it. Now we are back in the embrace, indeed in the womb, of a creative universe, capable of bringing forth life and even consciousness.

Evolution is not like the advance of the hands of a clock, moving relentlessly forward in fulfillment of preordained laws. Evolution is not fate; to evolve is not to meet one's destiny. We are not puppets on a cosmic stage, acting out a play whose script has been written and sealed. We are actors with will and purpose, and the power to vary the script—at least our part in it. We can vary it wisely or foolishly, to the extent of our wisdom—or our folly.

It was the best of times, it was the worst of times, it was the age of wisdom, it was the age of foolishness, . . . it was the spring of hope, it

173

was the winter of despair, we had everything before us, we had nothing before us. . . .

Thus wrote Charles Dickens in nineteenth-century England, in the turmoil of the first industrial revolution. He could have been writing of the world of the late twentieth century, in the grips of the second industrial revolution. For that much-bandied-about but little-known process, the progress of civilization, is not without its risks. It was with good reason that Alfred North Whitehead noted that the greatest advances in civilization have all but wrecked the societies that produced them. The technologies of information, communication, and automation, the torchbearers of societal evolution in our age, may yet wreck some contemporary societies— and the people who live in them.

Pessimism is premature; optimism is naive. Voltaire was right: the optimist believes that we live in the best of all possible worlds, and the pessimist is afraid that this is true. Neither does anything about it—the one because nothing *needs* to be done and the other because nothing *can* be done. The evolutionary realist knows that he can shape the world in which he lives—and he acts.

Modern science, it is said, has dethroned man, removing him from center stage and banishing him to a small planet in an indifferent solar system near the edge of a galaxy. But a grand synthesis of evolution enthrones man; it looks not at *where* we are but at *what* we are. We are one of the most remarkable expressions of nature's thrust toward order, structure, and system, toward the hazardous realms of nonequilibrium where survival calls for sophistication and skill—and ultimately for mind and intelligence.

Our new self-respect need not be exaggerated. We are surely among the evolutionary avant-garde, but we are not the highest-level system, even in our planetary environment. We are not the top of the evolutionary hierarchy, we are a part of larger systems. The global ecology—the quasi-living and breathing Gaia system— is the largest of the systems in our immediate environment. And within it there are innumerable smaller systems: ecologies, made up of plants, insects, and marine and terrestrial creatures of all kinds, as well as human societies, made up of ourselves and our fellow humans in a maze of intersecting and shifting relations.

Recognizing our "parthood" does not detract from our status as the most complex creature in this, and perhaps in any, region of the universe. And it does remove the anthropocentric blindfold that prevents us from seeing a great opportunity—and a grave threat. The opportunity is to consciously and purposively evolve society, the carrier of human evolution in our age. The threat is that the rapid evolution of increasingly complex structures in society may stifle the individual, locking him into relations that, while eminently functional in assuring dynamic stability in society, may be inhuman and constraining for its members.

To the best of our knowledge there is but one system in all the universe of which the parts are conscious while the whole is not, and that is human society. What is real wisdom and good ethics under these circumstances? If there should be a conflict between the welfare of the part and the evolution of the whole, should we not champion the former rather than promote the latter?

Evolutionary ethics is not necessarily the ethics of evolution. It could be the ethics of human freedom and creativity—the ethics of nurturing a faculty in the part even if it means putting a brake on the advance of the whole. Surely, if the part is one of the most noteworthy embodiments of the creativity of the cosmos, it has a right to some measure of self-interest.

Evolution, in cutting across time-honored but now antiquated disciplinary boundaries, contradicts common sense as much as modern physics ever did. Not only is the solid three-dimensional table on which I write a whirling dance of electrons and a vibrating symphony of molecules, but the electrons, atoms, and molecules of the universe are not fundamentally different from the tree outside the window and the dog by the fireplace. And none of them is fundamentally different from me and other human beings—nor from the technological society in which we live. Never has the classical French witticism *"Plus ça change plus c'est la même chose"* had as much meaning as it does today. To perceive only the diversity is obsolete common sense, and to perceive only the unity is pure mysticism. To perceive the unity within the diversity may be the higher sense, disclosed by the evolutionary vision.

For humanity, evolution is history. But history has been the prey of chance choices among alternatives, no less than subhuman or prehuman forms of evolution. History has been recorded, dissected, and debated ex post facto; it has not been studied and steered ante factum. Yet it can be so studied and steered: as evolution becomes history, it can become conscious. As Salk put it: conscious evolution can emerge from the evolution of consciousness—and the consciousness of evolution.

In a system such as contemporary society, evolution is always a promise and devolution always a threat. No system comes with a guarantee of evolution. The challenge is real. To ignore it is to play dice with all we have. To accept it is not to play God—it is to become an instrument of whatever divine purpose infuses this universe.

Hamlet's question is not whether to evolve or not to evolve, but whether to evolve with distinction or devolve to extinction. For the profound meaning of to be is to evolve, and evolution is liberal but not permissive: it does not let us stay fixed in our tracks, nor does it let us reverse our steps. But it does allow us to go forward as best or as poorly as we can.

"Know thyself" challenged the oracle at ancient Delphi. "Know how you evolve" is the challenge we face today.

In the beginning there was chaos, instability, inflation, and radiation. Within an almost infinitesimal fraction of a second the first microparticles evolved. After half a million years stable atoms—matter in the nonionized state—appeared. Within five billion years the galaxies began to take shape and the stars. In the last three billion years life emerged on earth. For the last quarter of a million years or so, hominid creatures with conscious minds roamed this planet. And for the past several thousand years we sapients have wondered: Where have we come from—and where are we going?

Today, some 20 billion years since the origins of the universe, we may be nearing the approach to the answer.

Appendix

The Ideal Scientific Theory:
A Thought Experiment

1. **The "cybernetics" of science.**[1] Does the growth of science have a recognizable direction in time? In the past, it was assumed that science converges toward greater fidelity of mapping of empirical phenomena, i.e. that it progresses toward "truth." Recently, however, the entire concept of truth has been rejected as unverifiable, and historical relativism emerged as a leading contender for the role of *theory of science*. The heuristic thesis of this study is that one does not have to take empirical truth as a criterion to distinguish an overall directionality in the growth of science, and that one can avoid the irrationality implicit in sociopsychological relativism without espousing any form of absolutism. Our thesis is that the development of science is governed by unchanging "controls" or "steering factors" which are specific to science as a human cognitive enterprise. The controls steer the process of theory construction, criticism and replacement. They are not reducible to a formal system of logic, nor are they undefinable matters of values and psychology. The controls can be specified, and the effect of their presence discerned in the history of science. By means of the resulting "cybernetics-of-science" concept of scientific growth, the indicated middle road can be pursued between historical relativism on the one hand and logical absolutism on the other. Ultimately, we must envisage science as a law-governed complex

Reprinted from *Philosophy of Science* 40, no. 1 (March 1973): 75–87.

system, tracing its own pattern of development over time. Such a conception does justice to the specific characterization of the scientific enterprise, and does not reduce it either to psychology and sociology, or to logic.

In science the closest approximations of invariant controls are known as "standards," "values," "ideals," or "internal steering factors."[2] The common referent of these terms is a set of science-constitutive principles in the light of which theories are formulated, criticized, compared, and selected. The principles do not require to be consciously entertained to be operative. In fact, it is safe to assume that the controls of scientific development are ideals which are practiced but seldom explicitly formulated.

Since we are dealing with science-constitutive control factors, we are not referring to principles derived from, or uniquely connected with, particular theories, frameworks, paradigms, or research programs. The controls are external to particular scientific formulations, but internal to science as an interpersonal historical-cognitive enterprise.

A visual approximation is helpful to achieve a preliminary grasp of the controls. For this purpose the reader is asked to envisage science as a structure consisting of systematically connected constructs (forming hypotheses, laws, principles, and mathematical relationships), rising in the vertical dimension above a horizontal plane. The latter bounds "nature" as the territory which is assumed to contain the objects referred to in the construct systems of science. Empirical facts lie where theory meets nature: there is no fact without theoretical conceptions, just as there is none without an observational content. The meeting of theory and nature defines the plane of observation and experiment: that is the realm of fact. Science rises above it to an extent determined by the level of abstraction and generality of its theories. For the vertical dimension constitutes the Platonic world of Ideas, the Whiteheadian world of Eternal Objects and the Popperian "third world." It is the conceptual field available for scientific exploration in regard to its applicability to facts.

The progress of science consists in the statistically irreversible movement of theoretical structures (henceforth called 'theories') with respect both to the realm of facts and the conceptual field. Theories tend to connect with nature on more and more points (i.e.

they discover and explain more facts), and they also tend to move or develop from the lower to the higher levels of the conceptual field. To account for these movements, we postulate two invariant controls which jointly exercise negative-feedback effects, steering science along a particular developmental pathway. (It is our expectation that this pathway coincides with that which can be read from a study of the history of science.)

One of the controls brings about movement in the horizontal direction. It prompts science to match its theories with nature on as many points as possible, with the highest attainable degree of precision. This control we may call the criterion (standard, value, steering factor) of *empirical adequacy*. The other control occasions movement in the vertical direction, from the lower to always higher levels of the conceptual field. It requires that scientists construct theories with the highest attainable level of integrated generality, making use of abstract (mainly mathematical) concepts to do so. We call this control the criterion (standard, value, steering factor) of *integrated generality*.

(i) Empirical adequacy leads science to discover single-valued invariances in the realm of facts. It probes in depth and in width a science's designated territory in nature, drawing initially on observations, and subsequently mainly on theory suggested measurements and experiments. Experimental rather than theoretical scientists respond to this control above all. They seek to map their territory, refine their maps, and increase their match with nature on all possible points. They adopt theories and assumptions as the situation may require. Thus alternative and possibly incommensurable hypotheses may be entertained in mapping out certain portions or aspects of a territory. Regardless of the consistency and elegance of the theoretical framework, the result is an increasingly precise map, taking into account and explaining with increasing precision a great number of facts.

(ii) A contrasting but not opposing control regulates tendencies in science to expand in the vertical dimension of generality and abstraction. Concern here is with the refinement of theory and not with the gathering of more empirical data (although the new theory may lead to new empirical discoveries). The control in question may be stated in the form of a requirement that the empirical base of a science (i.e., all the facts known to pertain to a given territory

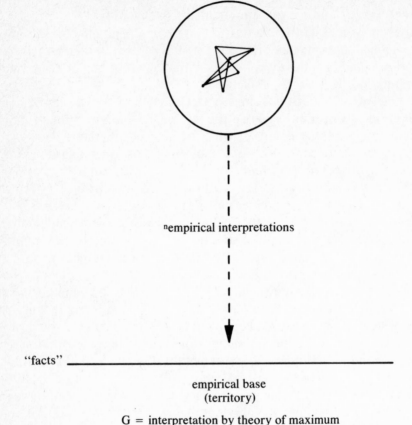

^{n}empirical interpretations

"facts" _____

empirical base
(territory)

G = interpretation by theory of maximum
consistency, elegance, and unity

Fig. 16

in nature) be explained by a theory of maximum consistency,
elegance and unity, i.e. containing the smallest number of existential postulates with no *ad hoc* assumptions. The requirement
selects toward a "minimal ontology" and is an application of
Occam's razor within science. If a theory is truly economical, its
basic terms become optimally general (have the greatest number of
empirical applications); it explains the most facts with the least
assumptions. Just how integrated and general theories in a science

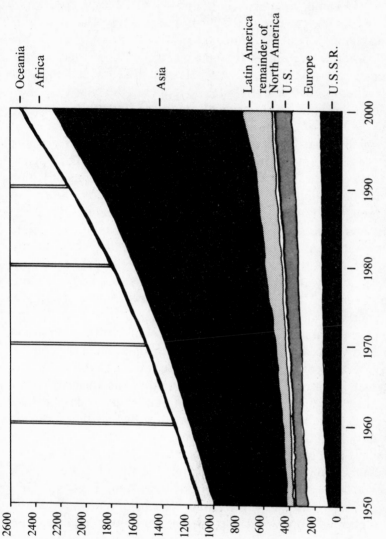

Fig. 17. *Labor Force Estimates and Projections: World Regions, 1950–2000*

SOURCE: From 1981 Statistical Yearbook, Dept. of Economic & Social Affairs, United Nations, 1983.

can become depends on the history of that science, its degree of dogmatism in its adherence to received paradigms, and the amount of innovative genius available for proposing alternative theories.

The vertical extension of a field is the work of theoreticians. Speaking as one of them, Einstein said, "we are seeking for the simplest possible system of thought which will bind together the observed facts" ([5], p. 138). And Heisenberg affirmed that, although contemporary scientists are no longer in the happy position of Kepler, who believed himself to be on the threshold of understanding the Plan of Creation, "the hope for a great interconnected whole which we can penetrate further and further remains the driving force of research for us too" ([7], p. 94). The logical unification of a plurality of lower level theories, by means of which nature can be exhibited as a great interconnected whole, more and more adequately known, is the chief research motivation of great theoreticians, who do not significantly add to the number of facts taken into account in a science, but integrate the facts already accounted for in a theory of higher level of generality, abstraction, and heuristic power. The work of Copernicus, Kepler, Newton, Darwin, Comte, Maxwell, Planck, Heisenberg, von Bertalanffy, and Wiener first and foremost provide internal consistency and unity on the given field, by pushing the level of theory further and further into the realm of abstraction. Of course, abstract-general unifying theories may prove to have excess empirical content, as Popper and Lakatos have shown. But neither the formulation of such theories nor their acceptance is predicated on empirical adequacy as the chief consideration. In fact, the predicted excess empirical content of general theories may be untestable at the time the theory is proposed, without this circumstance interfering either with their formulation or their acceptance. Examples are Dirac's hypothesis that electrons have antiparticles, and Einstein's hypotheses of gravitational waves. Both have been untestable at the time the theories from which they derive were postulated, yet the latter were found to have cogency independently of this fact.

2. The "target" of science: the ideal theory. If scientific growth is a self-regulative process, it has an intrinsic goal or "target" given by the focal point of the confluence of its controls. This does not make scientific progress a closed process, like the fulfillment of a plan, since the target is not known prior to reaching it and can only be deduced from patterns of development already realized. If such patterns can be discerned, scientific progress is neither random nor need it be governed by irrational or extraneous factors (shifting preferences of scientific communities, or "nature"). We have distinguished two principal controls regulating the growth of science, and we can now perform a simple thought experiment by extrapolating from past developments to the future, holding the controls constant. Thus we can discuss the "ideal scientific theory" (henceforth 'ideal theory') toward which science can be said to evolve. To predict the *content* of that theory produces the paradox that the prediction constitutes its own fulfillment: the possession of the ideal theory. But we can discuss the *form* of the ideal theory, and can offer an educated guess at its possible content, based on concepts currently emerging in the growing edge of theoretical science.

(a) The form of the ideal theory. The ideal theory is optimally adequate on the empirical plane: it describes, explains and predicts all describable, explainable, and predictable elements in nature in terms of invariant construct systems.[3] (Whether the set of thus explicable phenomena is equal to the set of all phenomena is undecidable unless it is demonstrated to be the case. For if any phenomenon refuses to yield to scientific treatment, we would never know whether it does so because it is either intrinsically incapable of such treatment; e.g. it is capricious, or else science has not yet succeeded in grasping it.) The descriptions, explanations, and predictions flow out of a theory that is optimally general and integrated as regards its primitive terms and their underlying assumptions. The ideal theory is logically that which reduces the number of primitive postulates to one. From this one postulate flow all statements referring to the set of scientifically knowable phenomena, and the deduced statements produce precise time and space invariant descriptions, explanations and predictions of the behavior of the set.

The single postulate of the ideal theory posits one most-general genus of entity which is both descriptively and dynamically analyzed. Its descriptive analysis results in the description of the basic structural properties of the universe. Since the relation between theory and phenomena is one-to-many, the phenomena are described as a hierarchy of recurrences of the basic entity. The entity recurs in as many transformations as there are levels in the hierarchy, and in as many variations on the transforms as there are members on each level. On the hierarchy's fundamental level of smallest size and least structure, the entity recurs in a large but finite number. On the highest level it recurs but once: the entity is then the universe as a whole. On intermediate levels the number of recurrences of the entity correlates with the level relative to the lowest and the highest: the levels and numbers increase and decrease inversely. The entity conserves its identity as the invariance of organizational form throughout the range of transformations, which correlate with each level as to species, and each member of each level as to individuals. Thus individually unique individuals are analyzed to particular transforms of a universal entity. Hereby concrete phenomena obtain optimally general explanation without the vagueness associated with qualitative generalities.

Dynamic analysis yields the patterns of change traversing the hierarchy. It is the same genus of entity that changes in transforms corresponding to different species, and individuals within the species. Since all transforms interact within the cones of causal propagation in space-time, the change of one transform is reflected in the change of a large number, and ultimately of all. Conversely, the change of every transform is ultimately reflected in the change of each. Hence the hierarchy forms a network with complex mutual causal pathways. Dynamic analysis discloses how any given transform changes under the influence of its own dynamic laws as conditioned by causal agencies propagated from the rest of the universe falling within its space-time cone, and how its change effects changes in all entities within the future dimension of the cone. Thus all changes observable in concrete phenomena are explained by dynamic laws governing change in nature as a whole.

(b) *The content of the ideal theory.* The content of the ideal theory is worked out in the long and possibly infinite process of growth, with various (but according to our cybernetic conception of development, damped) oscillations, that we group under the umbrella concept "the science of the future." Although no reliable predictions can be made as to the content of that theory, some guesses may be hazarded which constitute the best forecasts one can make from one phase of development to the next. This means taking the already emerged concepts of science and choosing among them those which best accord with the form of the ideal theory, and heuristically assuming that these concepts are capable of the indicated degree of development. This is what we shall do here as a thought experiment.

We know that the ideal theory explains the manifest diversity of empirical phenomena with the highest conceivable degree of accuracy and by deduction from the least number of assumptions about the universe. It thus explains diversity by tracing its evolution from common origins, in accordance with some general patterns of order. Now, the emergence of complex forms of diversity from relatively simple beginnings poses the problem, whether the laws that apply to the simpler forms also apply to (and are adequate to explain) the more complex. The ideal theory, of course, must include laws which are general enough to overcome a dualistic split in nature. We can extrapolate to some such laws by using Bronowski's recently advanced concepts of "stratified stability" [3]. These overcome the incipient vitalism of such writers as Polanyi, Elsasser and Wigner. Wigner [17], argues that organic reproduction is subject to so many statistical variations due to quantum effects that there can be no certainty that organisms could survive unless controlled by higher laws. Elsasser [6], calls for "biotonic" laws to explain the development of the organism since it is too complex to be controlled by physical laws encoded in the genes. Polanyi ([13], [14]), asserts the existence of some overall plan which directs the evolution of complexity: there can be no explanation of the phenomena of evolution without reference to a purpose. Just as the design of a watch can be understood only in reference to its purpose (to tell time), so the design of the mechanism of life can be understood only at the higher level of explanation given by purpose. This is the boundary condition for any mechanism. The argument advanced by Bronowski, and further extended here as a paradigm for an ideal theory, eliminates the pluralism inherent in these views and replaces it with a single process theory which accounts for hierarchically ordered diversity without practicing reductionism.

Consider the problem which is posed by the apparent contradiction between the second law of thermodynamics and the evolution of complexity. One could avoid it formally by saying that the second law applies only to isolated closed systems, and complex systems are open. But while this overcomes the contradiction between the second law and the emergence of complex systems, it does not *explain* the latter. For given a constant set of flows of energy, the range and frequency of variations in complexity can be set forth and particular peaks achieved; but these peaks could not be maintained. Most of the variants would fall back to the average almost immediately by the usual thermodynamic processes of degradation. How some complex arrangements can establish themselves, and form the matrix for the emergence of still more complex systems, remains a mystery. However, there has emerged in recent years a new branch of thermodynamics, namely irreversible (or nonequilibrium) thermodynamics, which studies the stability of flows far from equilibrium. Systems which maintain a stable pattern of flows far from equilibrium exist. They survive on an energy input which is dissipated in the maintenance of the structure. Prigogine and Katchalsky call them "dissipative structures" ([15], [8]). These differ from equilibrium structures, which require no input of energy to maintain. Classical thermodynamics is limited to the study of equilibrium structures and is thus incapable of explaining the endurance of complex systems far from equilibrium. However, such systems not only endure; they also evolve toward greater complexity, thus directly (though locally) reversing the direction of entropy. Enduring dissipative structures exist in stationary states, in which the balance of forces within the total configuration of the system does not degrade with time. Equilibria in the thermodynamic sense, on the other hand, is maintained on the principle of indifference: numerically the most configurations of the systems are bunched around it, and the system settles into it as its most probable state. Such states are "memoryless" in that their structure and function are not determined by the system's past history. However, nonequilibrium steady states are determined by the past history of the system. In fact, many such systems—like the class of biological phenomena—are thermodynamically extremely improbable according to the statistics of classical thermodynamics. (See [1].)

Presently, beginnings have been made in the understanding of stable systems far from equilibrium. Onsager, Prigogine, Meixner, de Groot, Katchalsky, and Curran have provided the basic equations for the balance of flows that maintains such systems in time ([4], [9], [12], [15]). Despite these achievements, nonequilibrium thermodynamics is presently limited to systems close to equilibrium and requires a linear relation between flows and forces. But biological (and conceivably *all* complex) systems are based on coupled reactions which are generally nonlinear and far from equilibrium. Such systems not only buffer out minor perturbations and return to their stationary state, but may, on prolonged disturbance, prove to be unstable and settle into a new internal balance of forces. That is, complex dissipative structures not only maintain themselves, but evolve in a changing environment. Basic models for these processes have been proposed by Turing and Prigogine ([15], [14]). In some cases it was feasible to identify stable regions beyond the realm of the existing stationary state. Katchalsky points out that it is "intriguing to speculate that further from equilibrium, in the far range of nonlinear phenomena, there exist still other stable stationary states the structure of which are as yet unknown" ([8], p. 116). Moreover, as he says, these stable potential states may explain the discontinuous transition from one nonequilibrium structure to another when accompanied by an input of energy. A stratified stability of potential levels may be the basis of the evolution of nonequilibrium systems.

Bronowski offers this hypothesis as a general cosmological principle. He assumes that there are relationships between ordered flows which are more stable than others and, when brought about by the chance shuffling of flows in the physical universe, constitute preferred configurations which do not degrade to the thermodynamical equilibrium state. Given chance shufflings of flows, the inherently stable preferred configurations will be sooner or later hit upon. These occasions may be extremely rare, but when they occur they present a level around which the chance play of fluctuations in the system's states can bunch as a new average. There develops a tug-of-war within the system between this level and the thermodynamical equilibrium average.

Since the average has no inherent stability, the preferred stable configuration will capture members of the system often enough to change the distribution; and, in the end, the system will be established at this level as a new average. In this way, local systems of a fair size can climb up from one level of stability to the next, even though the configuration at the higher level is rare. When the higher level becomes the new average, the climb is repeated to the next higher level of stability; and so on up the ladder of strata. ([3], pp. 33–34).

Consequently the arrow of time is given a barb which keeps it from running backward. Once it has this barb, the chance play of errors takes it forward of itself. Thus what we need to explain the phenomena of evolution in the cosmos is a complete nonequilibrium thermodynamics coupled with a statistical interplay of energies. Provided we have equations for all possible preferred configurations in nonequilibrium systems (the universe's potential "levels of stability") we can understand how simple systems cohere close to equilibrium yet not in it, and how such systems, upon further input of energy, can climb the levels of complexity one by one. The ideal theory, containing equations for all levels of stability as well as for the energy (and possibly information) flows which give the inputs for existing systems, links the physical, the biological, the ecological, and the psychosocial realms in a continuous multilevel sweep of projections. It explains how the chance configuration of hydrogen nuclei gives rise to a process which stabilizes in the form of a more complex helium nucleus; how helium nuclei combine with other elements in the energy shuffling processes of stellar evolution. It further explains how a few among the thus constituted atoms build the base configurations of biological systems (thymine, adenine, cytosine, and guanine) which are inherently stable and can build further stable assemblies (the nucleic acids). The theory continues to explain how stable genes are assembled from nucleic acids and how these synthesize the chemical building blocks of cells (proteins and enzymes). The ideal theory contains the equations for stable stationary states beyond the cellular level, showing a stable configuration for *all* potentially realizable multicellular organisms (existing and extinct species are but a fraction of this set). Moreover, stable configurations on the multiorganic level are likewise understood, and we get the set of realizable social and ecological systems. According to the ideal theory, the total potential of stability in the universe can be realized step by step, each higher level of realization resting on the one below it. Bronowski puts it picturesquely:

The stable units that compose one layer are the raw material for random encounters which will produce higher configurations, some of which will chance to be stable. So long as there remains a potential of stability which has not become actual, there is no other way for chance to go. It is as if nature were shuffling a sticky pack of cards, and it is not surprising that they hold together in longer and longer runs. ([3], p. 32)

The "stickiness" of the cards is the phenomenon which classical thermodynamics disregards and which the new nonequilibrium thermodynamics, here conceived as an integral part of the ideal scientific theory, accounts for. Accordingly we get an open-ended and unbounded process, going along one of a set of possible pathways, moved along by the chance play of errors. But, inasmuch as concepts of chance and randomness within a theory lower its level of empirical adequacy (compared with the exact numerical values flowing out of the application of dynamic laws), we must assume that the ideal theory will find a way to overcome resorting to chance and will replace stochastic laws with dynamic ones. Such a move does not render the described processes mechanistic, for the new dynamic laws need not be (and in fact are unlikely to be) laws of classical mechanics. Here we can take our cue from hypotheses suggested by Bohm [2].

Bohm suggests that there are entire hierarchies of order between random and mechanistic motion. The concept of order is the basic factor we need to understand. It is what unites mind and matter, the organic and the inorganic, and in fact all the diversity of phenomena in the empirical world. It is more fundamental than other notions, such as relationships and classes. What is required, according to Bohm, is the elaboration of a new mathematics capable of mapping hierarchies of order—the emergence of new orders based on variations of sequences of already established orders. He points out that there are certain natural hierarchies of order which reflect the existence of real structures; for example, elementary particles are ordered to make the atoms, atoms to make molecules, molecules to make micro-objects, and so on to the planets, stars, galaxies, and galaxies of galaxies. For living matter the molecules are ordered to make the components of cells; these are ordered to make the cells, these the organs, these the organisms, and these the societies of organisms ([2], pp. 22–23). And, Bohm adds, something similar goes on in perception and thinking. What is essential to process is not merely that there is a change of order and structure, but that the differences are similar, so that the changes are themselves ordered. Process is an order of change. Even the orders of change can be ordered to form a larger hierarchy of process, which is an order of orders of change. Evolution is the coming into being of a new and higher order of process. It leads to ever higher degrees of intrinsic determination of the order of lower orders' actions, so that it has a kind of direction of development.

If the basic motion of the particles which build the hierarchy of orders is mechanical, the entire hierarchy may be regarded as a conceptual abstraction. Reductionism can be practiced: what really exists can be said to be the particles as basic building blocks. However, if it turned out that natural processes cannot be reduced to mechanical order, these attempts would fail. It does seem most unlikely that the processes of evolution in any sphere of investigation would lend themselves to explanation by laws of mechanics applied to their smallest components. Already the laws of contemporary physics are not mechanistic: the subject matter of quantum theory is, as Bohm says, in certain ways more similar to that of biology than to the universe of Newtonian mechanics. Furthermore the laws of organization are not laws of the energy and behavior of individual components but are "social" laws of patterns of persistent configuration. The laws governing the behavior of particles do not seem sufficient *in principle* for the understanding of enduring configurations. Concepts such as entropy, feedback, the exclusion principle, stability far from equilibrium, and so on, are not laws of the behavior of particular components but that of the behavior of patterned assemblies. As Katchalsky points out, "It is not that the laws of assemblies are nonphysical or beyond the grasp of natural science—only that they are different and *cannot* be derived from the laws characterizing the behavior of single particles" ([8], p. 101). This fact calls for laws of complex non-equilibrium organization (systems laws, for example), and not for vitalism.

It may become evident, and be recognized in the ideal theory, that the laws of the physical universe itself are laws of patterned organization. What we now take as separate particles may in fact turn out to be organizations of underlying fields. Bohm says that it already appears to many physicists as if the beginning of an entirely new order of natural law were being revealed, in which the particles would be like the flowers on a carpet pattern, while there would be something as yet new and unknown, which corresponds to the woven structure of cords that constitute the carpet. So when we analyse the world as if it were made of particles, this might be similar to analysing a carpet as if it were made of the flowers that can be abstracted from its patterns. ([2], p. 36)

Given laws of organized assemblies, we may be able to avoid reference to purely random events. An inner logic, or emerging hierarchy of order, could characterize the processes of the universe. Randomness and chance appear if we concentrate on the particularities which are, in Bohm's metaphor, the flowers on the carpet. But when we understand the carpet, we get instead of randomness some extremely complex forms of order. Within the carpet—i.e. in the matrix of the physical universe—may lie those strata of stability which are being successively realized by the emerging configurations on which we now concentrate. The processes of the universe may be more like the unfolding of a complex yet nonrandom hierarchy of emergent order, coded by the inherent levels of potential stability within its matrix, than the chance interplay of energies and existing configurations. New orders would arise on the template of existing orders and would tend to produce still higher levels of emergent order. Thus the appearance of chance events could be replaced by a mathematics of orders of orders without making the universe mechanistically deterministic.

The ideal theory is assumed to possess a new mathematics which enables it to explain phenomena with the degree of precision associated with dynamic laws; it would not be ideal if it did not. It also contains the full set of equations for the possible stable configurations of complex systemic flows, and for the fields of energy and their interaction. It is ideal precisely because it can explain (predict as well as retrodict) all patterned processes of development in the universe with the highest degree of accuracy flowing from deductions from a core of assumptions of the highest level of integrated generality. Its structure can be reconstituted in the following scheme:

EXISTENTIAL ASSUMPTION
Hierarchy of stable nonequilibrium systems

EXPLANATORY HYPOTHESES
(i) Equations for all possible stable configurations
(ii) Equations for all energy fields and interactions

INSTRUMENTAL CONCEPTS
Mathematics of hierarchy of orders

EXPLANATIONS
Integrated descriptive and dynamic analyses
of nonequilibrium systems

By deduction from the assumption of a hierarchy of stable systems far from thermodynamical equilibrium, through the hypotheses containing equations for all possible stable configurations of energy flows and all energy fields and interactions, using the mathematics of a hierarchy of orders, the ideal theory can realize the basic goal of science: giving complete and integrated descriptive and dynamic analyses of the objects of its investigation. At present, descriptive analyses are possible mainly in regard to relatively simple physical systems, where the variables are simple enough, and can be sufficiently isolated, to permit the definition of the state space of the system. By contrast, dynamic analyses are the basic mode of explanation in the case of biological systems, where due to the complexity of the state variables it is useful (and, for the time being, necessary) to abstract from the structural details of the system and treat it as, in some respects, a black box. A complete understanding of a system presupposes, however, that complete structural (descriptive) and functional (dynamic) analyses are given, and that these are integrated thus that it becomes possible to infer the system's function from a knowledge of its structure, and determine its structure in reference to its function. The integrated description of the system shows the trajectory of the changes in the state space over time, i.e., shows how the system evolves. The evolution of systems is completely explained by the interaction of forces acting on the system and providing inputs to it, and the internal structure, on the basis of which the system responds (provides the output). In the ideal theory the structural explanations are furnished by identifying the system under investigation with one of the set of possible stable configurations of energy flows, and the functional explanations are given by identifying the energy and information inputs of the system from its environment and relating them to its structure. Thus by integrating the set of differential equations defining the system's state space with those which define its interactions with its environment, the ideal theory provides explanations of all present, past, or future states of the system when the required initial conditions are specified. This signifies an optimum degree of empirical adequacy. Inasmuch as it is attained by deduction from a theory of minimal existential assumptions and explanatory hypotheses, it conforms to the invariant ideals of science. It is in this sense, aside from all further considerations of categorical truth and certainty, that it is the ideal theory.

Conclusion. Our thought experiment has come to an end. The ideal scientific theory may never come about, nor is its achievement necessarily desirable. If, as Dewey emphasized, virtue is in the striving, and not in the final attainment, such a theory is a value as long as it is striven for and not when it is attained. Yet we can say with Plato that those who seek must have some knowledge of what they are after even if they do not possess it. The vital element in science, its progressive developmental character, can only be furthered by performing thought experiments on its ultimate goal— the one which, if reached, would negate the values implicit in striving for it. Thus speculations such as these, though far fetched, are not without their practical values. They specify the direction that science is moving, and can deduce the heuristics whereby such movement is facilitated.

NOTES

1. A detailed exploration of the cybernetic conception of scientific growth is proposed in the author's [10].
2. See, for example, Kuhn ("standards and values"), Margenau ("metaphysical requirements on constructs"), Törnebohm and Radnitzky ("internal steering factors"), Popper's ideas on the heuristic power of hypotheses, and Lakatos' concept of a progressive research program.
3. "Describes, explains and predicts" refers to an empirically adequate mapping of phenomena, where it is understood that description is low level explanation, and prediction is either description or explanation projected in time.

REFERENCES

[1] Bertalanffy, L. von. *Problems of Life*. New York: John Wiley, 1952.

[2] Bohm, D. "Some Remarks on the Notion of Order." In *Towards a Theoretical Biology*. Vol. II. Edited by C. H. Waddington. Chicago: Aldine Publishing Co., 1969.

[3] Bronowski, J. "New Concepts in the Evolution of Complexity: Stratified Stability and Unbounded Plans." *Zygon* 5 (1970): 33–34.

[4] De Groot, S. R., and Mazur, P. *Non-Equilibrium Thermodynamics*. Amsterdam: North Holland Publishing Co., 1962.

[5] Einstein, A. *The World As I See It*. New York: Covici-Friede, 1934.

[6] Elsasser, W. M. *The Physical Foundations of Biology*. Elmsford, New York: Pergamon, 1958.

[7] Heisenberg, W. *Philosophic Problems of Nuclear Science*. London: Faber and Faber, 1952.

[8] Katchalsky, A. "Thermodynamics of Flow and Biological Organization." *Zygon* 6 (1971).

[9] Katchalsky, A., and Curran, P. *Non-Equilibrium Thermodynamics in Biophysics*. Cambridge, Massachusetts: Harvard University Press, 1965.

[10] Laszlo, E. "A General Systems Model of the Evolution of Science." *Scientia* 107 (1972).

[11] Lefever, R., Nicolis, G., and Prigogine, I. "On the Occurrence of Oscillations around the Steady State in Systems of Chemical Reactions far from Equilibrium." *Journal of Chemical Physics* 47 (1967).

[12] Onsager, L. "Reciprocal Relations in Irreversible Processes." *Physical Review* 37 and 38 (1931).

[13] Polanyi, M. "Life Transcending Physics and Chemistry." *Chemical and Engineering News* 45 (1967).

[14] Polanyi, M. "Life's Irreducible Structure." *Science* 160 (1968).

[15] Prigogine, I. "Structure, Dissipation, and Life." In *Theoretical Physics and Biology*. Edited by M. Marois. Amsterdam: North Holland Publishing Co., 1969.

[16] Turning, A. M. "The Chemical Basis of Morphogenesis." In *Philosophical Transactions of the Royal Society of London* (1952).

[17] Wigner, E. P. "The Probability of the Existence of a Self-Reproducing Unit." In *The Logic of Personal Knowledge*. Edited by E. Shils. London: Routledge and Kegan Paul, 1961.

Notes

Chapter 2

1. In a condition of equilibrium the production of entropy, and forces and fluxes (the rates of irreversible processes), are all at zero, while in states near equilibrium entropy production is small, the forces are weak, and the fluxes are linear functions of the forces. Thus a state near equilibrium is one of *linear* nonequilibrium, described by linear thermodynamics in terms of statistically predictable behaviors, as the system tends toward the maximum dissipation of free energy and the highest level of entropy. Whatever the initial conditions, the system will ultimately reach a state characterized by the least free energy and the maximum of entropy compatible with its boundary conditions.

2. Change in the entropy of the systems is defined by the well-known Prigogine equation $dS = d_iS + d_eS$. Here dS is the total change of entropy in the system, while d_iS is the entropy change produced by irreversible processes within it and d_eS is the entropy transported across the system boundaries. In an isolated system dS is always positive, for it is unquely determined by d_iS, which necessarily grows as the system performs work. However, in an open system d_eS can offset the entropy produced within the system and may even exceed it. Thus dS in an open system need not be positive: it can be zero or negative. The open system can be in a stationary state ($dS = 0$), or it can grow and comlexify ($dS < 0$). Entropy change in such a system is given by the equation $d_eS = -d_eS \leq 0$); that is, the entropy produced by irreversible processes within the system is shifted into the environment.

3. A great deal of confusion surrounds the concepts of simplicity and complexity in contemporary scientific literature. Some investigators hold that simplicity and complexity are merely in the eyes of the beholder, that they are a feature of our descriptions and explanations of empirical phenomena, and not of the phenomena themselves. This is not the view taken here. Simplicity and complexity are considered a measure of the organizational structure of a real-world system. The measure provides information essential to our understanding of the nature and evolution of reality. It can be rendered operational by counting the number of parts in the system together with the connections between them, or by counting the number of "bits" of information that went into the construction of the system. The sciences of complexity are well named: not because they are more complex than their classical predecessors (indeed, they excel in the search for simplicity and elegance in theory

195

formulation and explanation), but because they deal with complex systems, and complex hierarchies of systems.

4. Free energy in a system is inversely related to entropy, as given by the equation $F = E - TS$ (where F is free energy, E is total energy, T is absolute temperature, and S is entropy). At any given temperature, the smaller the system's entropy, the greater its free energy, and vice versa.

5. There are two varieties of catalytic cycles: cycles of autocatalysis, in which a product of a reaction catalyzes its own synthesis, and cycles of cross-catalysis, in which two different products (or groups of products) catalyze each other's synthesis. An example of autocatalysis is the reactions scheme $X + Y \rightarrow 2X$. Starting from one molecule of X and one of Y, two molecules of X are catalyzed. The chemical rate equation for this reaction is $dX/dt = kXY$. When Y is held at a constant concentration there is an exponential growth in X. Cross-catalytic reaction cycles have been studied in detail by the school of Ilya Prigogine. A model of such reactions, known as the Brusselator, consists of the following steps:

$$
\begin{array}{ll}
(1) & A \rightarrow X \\
(2) & B + X \rightarrow Y + D \\
(3) & 2X + Y \rightarrow 3X \\
(4) & X \rightarrow E
\end{array}
$$

In this reaction model X and Y are intermediate molecules within an overall sequence through which A and B become D and E. In step (2) Y is synthesized from X and B, while in step (3) an additional X is produced through collisions of $2X$ and Y. Thus, while (3) in itself constitutes autocatalysis, (2) and (3) in combination make for cross-catalysis.

6. The empirical evidence for this process is indisputable. Diverse atomic elements converge in molecular aggregates; specific molecules converge in crystals and organic macromolecules; the latter converge in cells and the subcellular building blocks of life; single-celled organisms converge in multi-cellular species; and species of the widest variety converge in ecologies. As each level of organization is attained, evolution brings forth increasingly complex systems on that level. Atomic structures build in time from hydrogen to uranium and beyond; simple chemical molecules give rise to more complex polymers; organic species evolve from unicellular to multicellular forms, and immature ecologies build toward the mature climactic form. Continental ecosystems, which integrate vast and diverse populations in embracing energy-processing cycles, constitute the highest level (but by no means the most complex form) of organization in the biosphere.

7. The standard autopoietic model consists of five basic components: a "hole" (meaning an empty position in the grid of system interactions), a substrate, a simple link, a singly or fully bonded link, and a catalyst. Three basic transformations can be produced by these components: a catalyst and two substrate units can produce a link with a hole as a byproduct and leaving the catalyst unchanged; a free or bonded link can disintegrate into two substrate units and fill available holes; and various bonded links can be produced (a free link can be bonded with a bonded chain, two bonded chains can be bonded into one, or two free links can bond into a chain formation).

8. The theory states that if a process if controlled by some functional relation-ships (maximizing or minimizing functions), then the outcome of the changes can be explained by specific kinds of catastrophes. (The simplest catastrophe, the fold, has one control dimension and one behavior dimension, while a more complex catastrophe, the parabolic, has four control dimensions and two behavior dimensions.)

Chapter 3

1. Super-GUTs attempt to integrate all forces and interactions observed in the universe. They unify leptons and quarks, believed to be the basic elements of matter in the cosmos, by a gauge symmetry valid at very small distances (less than 10^{-16}cm). At larger distances the differences between quarks and leptons are assigned to a breaking of the symmetry. Two kinds of gauge symmetry are put forward to account for the unity of quarks and leptons. One, described by the group SU(5), consists of a family of fifteen fermions divided into two classes, of ten and five fermions respectively. The other symmetry, known as SO(10), is more stringent in that it relates all sixteen fermions to each other. Moreover, the parameters of the symmetry can be adjusted to match observ-able quantities. Another symmetry, relating fermions and bosons, turns out to be a form of supersymmetry: it postulates supersymmetric (and extremely heavy) "partners" to the observed leptons, quarks, and bosons. However, super-GUTs are as yet speculative. Fully developing the theory would mean integrating quantum theory into relativity theory, i.e., creating a quantum theory of gravity. This is a challenge that still awaits theoretical physicists.

2. It is interesting to note that this phase change corresponds remarkably to the process of bifurcation in nonequilibrium systems, i.e., to a basic feature of evolution *within* the cosmos. The sequence of states adds up to the phase portrait of an evolutionary bifurcation. (Compare with Figure 7 in Chapter 2.) There is an initial steady state which is destabilized and gives rise to a phase of chaos and indeterminacy; there is then a sudden leap into a new state through the amplification of some element in the randomly fluctuating sys-tem; and finally there is the emergence of a new and relatively stable dynamic regime which proves to be the initial state of a phase of progressive system building or self-complexification. The inflationary phase, like all processes of catastrophic bifurcation in evolving systems, separates the consequent phase from the initial phase: the nature of the observed order in the cosmos is not a function of whatever order may have reigned prior to inflation.

The interplay of determinism/indeterminism, and high/low entropy produc-tion correspond as well. There is a remarkable degree of order and determi-nism in the consequent phase, while chaos and indeterminism reign in the transitory chaotic phase. Entropy production reaches a maximum at the end of the inflationary state, as in all phases of bifurcation, and decreases as the new dynamic regime is established. If the evident similarity between the still speculative description of the very early universe and catastrophic bifurca-tions in nonequilibrium systems is not a superficial analogy or mere coinci-dence but a basic invariance at the root of reality, the processes of evolution *in* the cosmos repeat, in fact recapitulate, the evolutionary dynamic *of* the cosmos.

3. Prigogine and Géhéniau use the Landau-Lifshitz pseudotensors together with conformal (Minkowski) coordinates in their attempt to reconcile the evolution of the universe with the Einsteinian model. As this method suffers from the defect that, as a result of using the pseudotensors, it is not covariant, Prigogine and Géhénau propose a supplementary "C field" corresponding to the creation of matter in Einstein's field equation. The role of the C field is to express the coupling between gravitation and matter leading to the irreversible production of entropy. See I. Prigogine and J. Géhéniau, "Entropy, Matter, and Cosmology," *Proc. National Academy of Science* (U.S.A.) 83 (1986).

4. The exact time when galaxies began to form is still controversial: standard cosmological theories yield a figure for galactic mass that is far smaller than that indicated by observation. Some astrophysicists suggest that the universe may contain much "dark matter" (invisible to optical telescopes but registered by radio astronomy), such matter could have influenced the formation of galaxies and could account for the noted discrepancy.

5. More than fifty interstellar molecules have been identified so far, many with molecular weights exceeding fifty atomic mass units. Astrophysicists have also observed nearly two hundred additional unidentified features in the relevant millimeter-wave spectrum, while new detection techniques revealed the presence of amino acids as well as nucleic acids in meteorites.

6. Astronomer Frank Drake proposed an equation to calculate the number of civilizations in our galaxy that have the technology and the motivation to communicate with us. It is $N = R^* f_p n_e f_l f_i f_c L$. Here R equals the rate at which stars form. This is multiplied by the fraction of stars with planets, times the average number of planets physically capable of supporting life, times the fraction of the planets that actually give rise to life, times the fraction of life-supporting planets that generate intelligence, times the fraction of intelligent species that have the technology and the motivation to communicate, times the average life expectancy of civilizations that attempt communication. If we are interested simply in the occurrence of life, the probabilities increase sharply. Assuming the nonaccidental emergence of life (i.e., that all planets physically capable of supporting life actually give rise to life), the indicated equation is $N = R^* f_p n_e$: the rate of star formation times the fraction of stars with planets times the average number of planets that can physically support life.

7. The relevant equations are the following:
   (1) Cosmic background radiation:

Temperature	$T = 2.7 \pm 0.1$K;
Energy density	$u = a(2.7)^4 \cong 10^{-13}$ ergs cm^{-3},
where	a is the "radiation constant":
	7.6×10^{-15} erg cm^{-3} K^{-4}.

   (2) As $u \propto T^4$,

   the change of radiation temperature with time is:
   $$T = 2.7(1 + z) \cong 10^{10} t^{-1/2},$$

where	$z = v/c$,
	v is recessional velocity,
	c is speed of light,
and	t is given in seconds.

(3) Present 'equivalent' energy density of matter:
$$\rho_m c^2 \sim 10^{-8} \text{ erg } cm^{-3}.$$
(4) The temporal variance of the density of matter:
$$\rho_m 10^6 \, t^{-2}.$$
(5) The average temperature of matter at any time t:
$$T \cong 6 \times 10^{16} \, t^{-1},$$
(6) The average temperature of radiation at any time t:
$$T \cong 10^{10} \, t^{-1/2},$$
(7) The energy density of radiation [from (2)]:
$$aT^4.$$
(8) The energy density of matter [from (3)]:
$$\rho_m c^2;$$
(9) Temporal change in the proportion of energy density in matter and in radiation:
   when $t < 500,000$ years: $\rho_m c^2 < aT^4$;
   when $t = 500,000$ years: $\rho_m c^2 = aT^4$;
   when $t > 500,000$ years: $\rho_m c^2 > aT^4$;

For details see the appendix to Eric Chaisson, *The Life Era: The Role of Change in the Natural Universe* (Boston: Atlantic Monthly Press, 1987).

8. The cosmic evolution of matter stretches to an infinite time horizon if the universe is open—that is, if the mass of matter created in the course of time does not exceed the critical value of approximately 10^{-30} gram/cm³. Above this value the universe will contract back and end in a terminal Big Crunch; below it it will expand forever. Current measurements are not yet sufficiently refined to decide the exact value of matter density in the cosmos, hence we still cannot tell whether we live in an open or in a closed universe.

Chapter 4

1. In the classical account, natural selection acts on essentially random mutations. Mutations are "typing mistakes" in the repetition of the genetic code of the parent in the offspring, produced by all species at a more or less constant rate. Most of the mutants produced by chance variations are faulty in some respect and are eliminated by natural selection. However, random mutations occasionally hit upon a genetic combination that renders the individual more rather than less fit to live and reproduce. It transmits its mutant genes to successive generations, and the comparatively numerous offspring produced by these generations deplace the previously dominant species. The range of possible variations is constrained only by the comparative fitness of the mutants for life and reproduction in their habitats.

2. For example, a generalist species such as the *Aepycerotini* (of which the living member is the impala) seems to have survived the last six million years with only one or two speciations. But the more specialized *Alcelaphini* (which includes hartebeests and wildebeests) has undergone as many as twenty-seven speciations during the same period: changing system-environment relations kept knocking out the specialized populations from their narrow environmental ruts and replacing them with others more fitted to the new niche structures.

3. Genomes, consisting of nucleic acids (mainly DNA and RNA), perform numerous functions including self-replication, recombination, self-regulation and self-repair, and the synthesis of messenger RNA for the formation of proteins. All functions are coded by sequences of four nucleotides (adenine, guanine, cytosine, and thymine for DNA, and uracil instead of thymine for RNA) folded as a double helix inside the nucleus.

Chapter 5

1. A number of social scientists have tried to identify the nature of bonds in modern societies. Emile Durkheim suggested "social facts" and "solidarity" as explanatory concepts; Max Weber pioneered attempts to pin down the binding force of institutions in the social roles played by individuals, while Kurt Lewin produced actual measurements of such forces in terms of quasi-physical factors such as vectors, boundaries, and barriers. Likewise the experiments of Solomon Asch and Stanley Milgram contribute to the clarification of the nature of social bonds by identifying and measuring the operation of social constraints in terms of conformity and authority.

2. For example, a comprehensive report to the National Science Foundation defined technology as "any tool or technique, any physical equipment or method of doing or making, by which human capability is extended." L. G. Tornatzky et al., *The Process of Technological Innovation: Reviewing the Literature* (Washington, D.C.: National Science Foundation, 1983).

3. Technology as agent of social change leads neither to optimum energy efficiency nor to maximum energy consumption. In some sense consumption is the inverse of efficiency: the more energy one consumes to perform a given task, the less efficient one is. Of course, the energy requirement of the tasks performed in societies tends to grow as well. But as more energy-intensive tasks are adopted, energy efficiency can actually decrease. This was the case in the shift from preindustrial to industrial society. Energy consumption per capita went up, parallel with energy waste. By contrast the shift from industrial to postindustrial society decreases energy consumption per capita by increasing the efficiency with which energy is employed.

   Taken separately, neither energy efficiency nor gross energy consumption is the critical measure. That measure is the overall increase in the dynamism of society, i.e., the amount of free energy actually used to maintain the social system together with its population, its implements, and its infrastructure. If the accessed free-energy flux is abundant, consumption tends to go up and efficiency tends to go down. If the flux is dense rather than abundant, efficiency increases. While in history, energy consumption and efficiency fluctuate, often inversely, the energy used to maintain the social system shows an overall increase. There is a growth in the dynamism of society and therewith in its autonomy in the natural environment.

Chapter 6

1. It is possible, and may prove to be fruitful, to investigate these patterns in depth and show that the similarities between the evolution of matter-energy systems in the empirical world and the evolution of conceptual systems in

science are more than mere analogies. A model of scientific development could be proposed where theories are dynamic systems of constructs in interaction with their environment, consisting of other theories and theory developments, and the direct or indirect observation of "nature." Paradigms would represent the set of attractors that define the state of the construct system. During standard phases of "normal science," the attractors are stable (periodic or static) and regulate the development of the system of constructs in a deterministic manner. In periods of major innovation ("revolutions"), the attractors turn chaotic, and there are catastrophic bifurcations in the course of which attractors that define the outgoing paradigm disappear and those that define the incoming paradigm appear "out of the blue" (through the genius of innovators and the serendipity of the spread of their ideas). If such models prove to be reasonably accurate and dependable representations of the dynamics of theory elaboration and innovation, the development of science would appear as a genuine evolutionary process, and the applications of GES would be extended to the history, sociology, and philosophy of science.

2. In terms of the technologies of artificial intelligence, consciousness (and by this I mean the self-reflective, self-analytical capacity of the mind and not the basic phenomenon of feeling and sensation) is the functional equivalent of a subsystem designed to monitor the functioning of another system. The basic data of the subsystem are the signals passing to and fro among the elements of the host system. The monitor analyzes these data according to algorithms wired into its circuits. There may be subsidiary monitors that analyze data flows in the primary monitor. If a sequence consisting of a large number of monitors were to be built into an artificial system, the system would model the functional aspects of human consciousness.

Chapter 9

1. I am grateful to Robert Artigiani for supplying me with the pertinent historical data.

Bibliography

Nonequilibrium Thermodynamics and Dynamic Systems Theory

Abraham, Ralph, and C. Shaw. *Dynamics: The Geometry of Behavior*. Santa Cruz: Aerial Press, 1984.

Eigen, Manfred, and P. Schuster. *The Hypercycle: A Principle of Natural Self-Organization*. New York: Springer, 1979.

Epstein, Irving; K. Kustin; P. de Kepper; and M. Orban. "Oscillating Chemical Reactions." *Scientific American,* March 1983.

Glansdorff, P., and I. Prigogine. *Thermodynamic Theory of Structure, Stability and Fluctuations*. New York: Wiley Interscience, 1971.

Katchalsky, Aharon. "Biological Flow Structures and Their Relations to Chemo-diffusional Coupling." *Neuroscience Research Progress Bulletin* 9 (1971).

————, and P. F. Curran. *Nonequilibrium Thermodynamics in Biophysics*. Cambridge, Mass.: MIT Press, 1965.

Maturana, Humberto R., and Francisco Varela. *Autopoietic Systems*. Report BCL 9.4. Urbana: Biological Computer Laboratory, University of Illinois, 1975.

Nicolis, G., and I. Prigogine. *Self-Organization in Non-Equilibrium Systems*. New York: Wiley Interscience, 1977.

Onsager, L. "Reciprocal Relations in Irreversible Processes." *Physiological Review* 38 (1931).

Prigogine, Ilya. *Etude thermodynamique des phénomènes irreversibles*. Liège: Desoer, 1947.

————, and J. Géhéniau, "Entropy, Matter, and Cosmology," *Proc. National Academy of Science* (U.S.A.) 83 (1986).

————, and Isabelle Stengers. *Order Out of Chaos: Man's New Dialogue with Nature*. New York: Bantam, 1984.

The Science and Praxis of Complexity. Tokyo: United Nations University, 1985.

Thom, René. *Structural Stability and Morphogenesis*. Reading, Mass.: Benjamin, 1972.

Varela, Francisco; H. R. Maturana; and R. Uribe. "Autopoiesis: The Organization of Living Systems, Its Characterization and a Model." *Bio-Systems* 5 (1974).

Zeeman, Christopher. *Catastrophe Theory*. Reading, Mass.: Benjamin, 1977.

General and Evolutionary Systems Theory

Bertalanffy, Ludwig von. *General System Theory*. New York: Braziller, 1968.

Boulding, Kenneth E. *Ecodynamics: A New Theory of Societal Evolution*. Beverly Hills and London: Sage, 1978.

Corning, Peter A. *The Synergism Hypothesis: A Theory of Progressive Evolution.* New York: McGraw-Hill, 1983.
Gray, William, and Nicolas Rizzo (eds.). *Unity through Diversity.* 2 vols. New York: Gordon & Breach, 1973.
Haken, Hermann. *Synergetics.* New York: Springer, 1978.
———— (ed.). *Dynamics of Synergetic Systems.* New York: Springer, 1980.
Hayek, Friedrich A. von. *Kinds of Order in Society.* Studies in Social Theory No. 5. Menlo Park: Institute for Humane Studies, 1975.
Jantsch, Erich. *Design for Evolution.* New York: Braziller, 1975.
————. *The Self-Organizing Universe.* Oxford: Pergamon Press, 1980.
————, and Conrad H. Waddington (eds.). *Evolution and Consciousness.* Reading, Mass.: Addison-Wesley, 1976.
Laszlo, Ervin. *Introduction to Systems Philosophy.* New York: Harper & Row, Torchbooks, 1973.
Margenau, Henry (ed.). *Integrative Principles of Modern Thought.* New York: Gordon & Breach, 1972.
Pattee, Howard (ed.). *Hierarchy Theory: The Challenge of Complex Systems.* New York: Braziller, 1973.
Salk, Jonas. *The Anatomy of Reality.* New York: Columbia University Press, 1984.
————. *The Survival of the Wisest.* New York: Harper & Row, 1973.
Weiss, Paul A., et al. *Hierarchically Organized Systems in Theory and Practice.* New York: Hafner, 1971.

Biological Evolution

Ager, D. V. *The Nature of the Stratigraphic Record.* New York: John Wiley, 1973.
Carson, H. L. "The Genetics of Speciation at the Diploid Level." *American Naturalist* 109 (1975).
Corliss, John B. *On the Creation of Living Cells in Submarine Hot Spring Flow Reactors.* Proceedings, Fifth ISSOL Meeting and Eighth International Conference on the Origin of Life, Berkeley, Calif., 1986.
Csanyi, Vilmos. "General Theory of Evolution." *Studia Biologica Hungarica* 18. Budapest: Akadémiai Kiadó, 1982.
Denton, Michael. *Evolution: Theory in Crisis.* London: Burnett Books, 1986.
Eldredge, Niles. *Time Frames.* New York: Simon & Schuster, 1985.
————. "Stability, Diversity and Speciation in Paleozoic Epeiric Seas." *Journal of Paleontology* 48, no. 3 (1974).
————, and Stephen J. Gould. "Punctuated Equilibria: An Alternative to Phylogenetic Gradualism." In Schopf, ed., *Models in Paleobiology.* San Francisco: Freeman, Cooper, 1972.
————, and Stephen J. Gould. "Punctuated Equilibria: the Tempo and Mode of Evolution Reconsidered." *Paleobiology,* 3, 1977.
Gould, Stephen J. *Ever Since Darwin.* New York: W. W. Norton, 1980.
————. "Darwinism and the Expansion of Evolutionary Theory." *Science* 210 (1980).
————. Ontogeny and Philogeny. Cambridge, Mass.: Harvard, 1977.
Holling, C. S. "Resilience and Stability of Ecosystems." In Jantsch and Waddington, eds., *Evolution and Consciousness.* Reading, Mass.: Addison-Wesley, 1976.
Lotka, A. J. *Elements of Physical Biology.* Baltimore: Williams & Witkins, 1925.

Morowitz, H. J. *Energy Flow in Biology*. New York: Academic Press, 1968.
Oparin, A. I. *The Origin of Life*. New York: Macmillan, 1938.
Stanley, S. M. *A Theory of Evolution above the Species Level*. Proceedings of the National Academy of Sciences USA 72, 1975.
Volterra, V. *Leçons sur la théorie mathématique de la lutte pour la vie*. Paris: Gauthier-Villars, 1931.

Cosmic Evolution

Chaisson, Eric J. *Cosmic Dawn: The Origin of Matter and Life*. Boston: Atlantic, Little, Brown, 1981.
————. *The Life Era: The Role of Change in the Natural Universe*. Boston: Atlantic Monthly Press, 1987.
Hawking, S. W.; G. W. Gibbons; and S. T. C. Siklos, eds. *The Very Early Universe*. Cambridge: Cambridge University Press, 1983.
National Academy of Sciences–National Research Council. *Astronomy and Astrophysics for the 1980s*. Washington, D.C.: National Academy Press, 1982.
Trefil, J. S. *The Moment of Creation: Big Bang Physics*. New York: Scribners, 1983.

Index

207